The New Entrepreneur's Guide to Setting Up and Running a Successful Business

T0270969

The New Entrepreneur's Guide to Setting Up and Running a Successful Business

By Paul Kendall

CRC Press
Taylor & Francis Group
Boca Raton London New York

CRC Press is an imprint of the
Taylor & Francis Group, an **informa** business

A PRODUCTIVITY PRESS BOOK

CRC Press
Taylor & Francis Group
6000 Broken Sound Parkway NW, Suite 300
Boca Raton, FL 33487-2742

First issued in paperback 2020

© 2018 by Taylor & Francis Group, LLC
CRC Press is an imprint of the Taylor & Francis Group, an Informa business

No claim to original U.S. Government works

ISBN-13: 978-1-138-49869-3 (hbk)
ISBN-13: 978-0-367-73430-5 (pbk)

Library of Congress Cataloging-in-Publication Data

Names: Kendall, Paul (Paul Francis) author.
Title: The new entrepreneur's guide to setting up and running a successful business / Paul Kendall.
Description: New York : Taylor & Francis, [2018] | Includes bibliographical references and index.
Identifiers: LCCN 2018002451 (print) | LCCN 2018015987 (ebook) | ISBN 9781351015875 (eBook) | ISBN 9781138498693 (hardback : alk. paper)
Subjects: LCSH: New business enterprises. | New business enterprises--Management. | Accounting. | Advertising.
Classification: LCC HD62.5 (ebook) | LCC HD62.5 .K446 2018 (print) | DDC 658.1/1--dc23
LC record available at https://lccn.loc.gov/2018002451

Visit the Taylor & Francis Web site at
http://www.taylorandfrancis.com

and the CRC Press Web site at
http://www.crcpress.com

I would like to dedicate this book to my wife Sue, and to my children Nicola, Paul and Steven.

I would also like to thank and acknowledge all those I have had the privilege of working with during my career, and to the clients who provided me with the inspiration to write this book.

My thoughts are with those who did not fare so well, but provided me with the experience to forewarn others of the obstacles that may await them.

Contents

Preface xv

Author xvii

1 Introduction 1

The Aim of This Book 2

Who Will Be Interested in This Book? 2

New Business Startups 2

Government Assistance for New Businesses 4

Success Stories 6

Out of Acorns Giant Oaks Grow 6

   eBay and PayPal 6

   Starbucks 7

   Panasonic 8

   Apple 9

2 So You Want to Run Your Own Business 11

Why Are You Setting Up a Business? 11

   Viagra 12

   Evolution 12

   Unemployment 13

   You Can Do It Better 13

   A Eureka Moment 14

      The Post-it Note 14

      Velcro 15

   Technological Developments 15

   Developing an Idea 16

Vanity...17
You Want to be Rich 17
What Is Your Business Going to Do?...............18
Unique Selling Point 18
Where Should You Set Your Business Up (Both
Virtually and Actually)?....................................19
When Should You Start Your Business? 20
Who Should You Go into Business With?..........21
The Dasslers 21
Work as a Team..22
What Should You Call Your Business? 23

3   How Do You Start?...................................25
The Business Plan..25
Create a Brand, Logo and Business Design.......26
Sole Trader, Limited Company or Partnership?.................27
Sole Trader.. 28
Limited Company (Incorporation) 29
Partnerships 31
Budgeting and Cash Flow..................................33
Pricing and Costings 39

4   Buying and Selling a Business 43
Is the Price Right?...45
Value-Added Tax on a Transfer of a Business.................47
How Should You Finance the Purchase?............49
Crowdfunding 52
Tax Issues to Consider......................................54
What Records Should You Inspect?...................54
Buying a Franchise 55
How Will the Purchase of a Business Affect
Your Tax Bill? 57
Is the Business Right for You or Should You
Consider the Alternatives?................................57
Is the Split of the Purchase Price Right? 58
Should You Form a Limited Company to Buy a
Business?...58

Selling the Business 59
Selling an Incorporated Business 59
UK Enterprise Investment Schemes 60
    Enterprise Investment Scheme...................................61
    Capital Gains Tax Deferral Relief 62
    Inheritance Tax (IHT) Exemption 63
    Seed Enterprise Scheme....................................63
    SEIS Reinvestment Relief and Capital Gains Tax Relief 64

5 Staffing 65
Setting Wage Levels 66
Staff Pensions 67
Self-Employed Subcontractors 68
The National Minimum Wage 69
    Employment Legislation................................70
    Employers' Liability 70
    Staff Management...71
    Staff Relationships 71
    Statutory Maternity, Paternity, Adoption and
    Shared Parental Pay..72
    Statutory Sick Pay (SSP)....................................73
    Redundancy Pay...74
The Gig Economy 78
Contracts of Employment 79
Pro Forma Employment Contract...............................81
Pro Forma Freelance Agreement 86

6 Taxes and VAT...91
Income Tax...92
    Tax on Dividends..96
    Optimum Tax Planning for Directors on Low
    Earnings..96
Corporation Tax 97
Example of Tax Planning Exercise..............................98
    Year One...99
    Year Two..100
    Year Three..100

Value-Added Tax 102
  Current VAT Rates 103
Capital Gains Tax 103
  Capital Gains Tax Basic Rules 104
  Capital Gains Tax Rates and Bands 105
  Capital Gains Tax for People Non-Domiciled
  in the UK 106
Annual Tax on Enveloped Dwellings (ATED) 106
Stamp Duty Land Tax 107
Entrepreneurs' Relief 108
Capital Allowances 110
National Insurance 110
Inheritance Tax 111
Agricultural Relief 113

7 Accounts 115
Why Do You Need to Prepare Accounts? 115
What Accounting Records Do You Need to Keep? 116
Bookkeeping and Management Accounts 119
What Do the Accounts Look Like? 121
  Income 121
  Expenses 123
What Level of Profit Will You Make? 128
What Should You Do to Protect Your Income? 128
Tax Enquiries 129
The Balance Sheet 130
Fixed Assets 131
Goodwill 131
  Goodwill Valuations 132
Property 133
  What Type of Property Is Best for Your Business? 134
  Freehold or Leasehold: Should You Buy or Rent? 135
  Sale and Leaseback of Property and Gearing 138
  Who Should Own the Property? 140
  Do You Need a Property Ownership Agreement? 140
  How Do You Finance or Refinance the Property? 141

Negative Equity and Valuations 143
Basis of Valuation 144
Life Insurance and Endowments 144
Critical Illness and Health Insurance 145
Fixtures and Equipment 147
Motor Vehicles 148
Current Assets 149
    Stock 149
    Debtors 151
    Credit Card Facilities 152
    Debtors (Work in Progress and Prepayments) 153
    Cash at Bank and in Hand 153
Current Liabilities 154
Long-Term Liabilities 155
Purchase of Assets and Equipment: Cash, Hire
Purchase or Lease? 156
Annual Percentage Rate 159
    Working Out the Leasing Deal APR 160
    Excessive APRs on Payday Loans 162
Net Assets 164
Funding of Business Accounts 164
    Capital Accounts 166
    Current Accounts 167
    Drawings and the Payment of Tax 168
Accountants 169
How Do You Find a Good Accountant? 169
What Should You Expect from Your Accountant? 171
Legal Advisors 172
Solicitors, How Do You Find a Good One? 172
What Should You Expect from Your Solicitor? 172
The Annual Review Meeting 172

8 Promoting Your Business 175
The Business Website 175
Return on Investment 177
Mailings 178

E-mail Campaigns 179

Social Media 179

Blogging 180

Press Releases.. 180

Advertising... 180

Subcontract Web Content 181

Sponsorship and Publicity Stunts 181

Organize Contests or Free Gifts 182

Joint Marketing.. 182

Other Marketing Methods.. 183

Geo-Marketing 184

Impulse Buying.. 185

Push and Pull Marketing... 186

Discounts... 187

Networking... 187

**9 Now You've Got a Successful Business:
   What's the Next Step? 189**

Extra Outlets 189

Franchising 190

Fine-Tuning the Business... 191

Cost Cutting... 192

Reviewing Sales Promotions and Marketing
Campaigns 193

10 How It Can Go Horribly Wrong 197

Major Reasons for Insolvencies 197

Other Reasons for Failure... 200

Insolvency and Liquidators.. 201

Voluntary Arrangements.. 202

Draft Example of a Company Voluntary
Arrangement (CVA) Proposal... 203

   Introduction (Rule 1.3(1)) 203

   Proposals (Rule 1.3(2)) 206

      Secured Creditors 209

      Preferential Creditors.. 209

      Deferred Creditors 210

Unsecured Creditors 210

Associated Creditors 211

Alterations to the Proposal (Rule 1.3(3)) 215

Realization of Assets 215

Index to Appendices 216

Schedule 1 217

Schedule 2 218

Schedule 3 218

Schedule 4 219

Schedule 6 219

Schedule 7 221

Register of Charges 222

The Process of Insolvency 223

Outcomes Other than Voluntary Arrangements 223

Examples of Disasters 224

Indications of Poor Performance 225

Wrongful and Fraudulent Trading 226

Chasing Sales 227

11 Retirement and Succession 229

Passing the Business on to the Family upon
Death or Retirement 229

Retirement and Pensions 231

Individual Savings Accounts (ISAs) 232

Pensions 233

Increase in the State Pension Age 233

Annuities 236

Income Drawdown 236

Annuities Explained Further 237

Drawdown Explained Further 238

Tax Relief on Pension Contributions 238

Different Types of Pensions 239

Financial Advisors 240

NEST 241

Old Pensions 241

What Is the Best Retirement Date? 241

Investing in Someone Else's Business: What to Expect.....242
What Are You Looking for from the Investment?...........243
How Much to Invest? 244
The Pros and Cons of Investing in Privately
Owned Businesses..245

12 Essentials to Take Away......................................249
The Customer Should Always Come First......................249
Personal Complaints Line 249
Be the Best...250
Incorporate...250
It's a Team 250
Don't Have a Plan B 250
It'll Work… Think Positively...250
Don't Ever Assume Things 251
Attention to Detail..251
React to Change 251
Don't Ignore the Financials 252
Do It for Yourself 252
Take Advice..252
Get Insured 252
Start Your Pension Early 253
What Makes a Successful Business? 253
Business Plan 253

Index 273

Preface

A one-stop shop for the new business owner, this book provides the answers to the problems that business owners often come across.

Written by an accountant who has experience in dealing with thousands of successful and unsuccessful businesses, this book will prove invaluable to anyone considering starting their own business.

Also, it will be very useful to anyone studying a business course and provide them with a practical knowledge that academics would find hard to match.

The book has been written by an accountant with experience of dealing with UK businesses; however, the issues covered will apply to small businesses setting up anywhere in the world.

The book is not intended to be a global reference book in respect of business tax and legislation, but one that deals with the practical issues that businesses come across every day.

Avoid the pitfalls – buy the book!

Author

 **Paul Kendall** gained a degree in accountancy and financial management from Loughborough University in 1981, and subsequently went on to qualify as a Chartered Accountant in 1986.

He set up a niche practice advising businesses in the medical and dental sectors, and formed a national association of accountancy and legal businesses advising those sectors. He remained chairman of that association for many years.

He has written specialist books providing taxation and accountancy advice for businesses and professional practices.

Prior to the setting up of the niche practice, he had spent some time working in the insolvency department of an international firm of accountants, where he was able to assist failing businesses.

He retired at age 51, to look after his investments and spend his time between his holiday homes in Switzerland, Spain and the UK.

Chapter 1

Introduction

If you're reading this, you are seriously considering setting up your own business, and you've got lots of questions that need answers. This book should provide you with most of the answers you need, and save you thousands in professional fees.

This book will also help prevent you falling into the traps that many unsuccessful businesses have found themselves caught up in. It's not an easy job to grow a successful small business, and it's for that reason I have included a few cautionary notes to stop you wasting what little time and money you have.

With regard to your planned business startup, the figures are stacked against you before you start, as 90% of new businesses fail! Read on and let's see what we can do to ensure your business becomes one of the 10% that make it.

Even if you don't make it on your first attempt (as you're not a quitter, you'll try again!), what you learn from this book will ensure that your dreams will become reality somewhere down the line.

The Aim of This Book

The aim of this book is to provide you, the new business owner, with sufficient knowledge to successfully run your own business. It also aims to provide you with an insight into the level of knowledge of taxation, general management and the legal framework that you will need to successfully grow your business.

Who Will Be Interested in This Book?

Although this book will be of interest to those already running their own business, it has been written primarily for the benefit of those planning to set up a new business.
Much of the content relates to business owners operating as

Sole traders
Expense-sharing arrangements
Partnerships
Limited companies

The distinction between these different arrangements and the tax and legal considerations of each will be explained in full in Chapter 3.

New Business Startups

I have already referred to the high level of failure in business startups. To give you a further insight into the failure rate, I would like to add some information from the Small Business Administration in the USA regarding the longevity of new business startups.
    They discovered that 7 out of 10 new businesses survive at least 2 years, half at least 5 years, a third at least 10 years and a quarter last 15 or more years.

However, this doesn't appear to have dampened the desire of entrepreneurs to try, as the number of new businesses continually being set up is phenomenal.

There are always entrepreneurs who will continue to identify and take advantage of every opportunity available to make a profit, with a staggering 100 million businesses launched worldwide each year.

In the 10 minutes or so that you've taken to read to this point, over 1900 new businesses have been created, and sadly over 1710 new businesses will have ceased trading.

This high level of failure does not put off those who wish to start their own business, as the desire to set up in business, especially among people in their twenties and thirties, has increased significantly in the last few years. Figures that I have obtained from Companies House in the UK of new businesses that recently incorporated clearly show this trend (Table 1.1).

The number of new company registrations in the UK in 2017 to date (July 2017) exceeds 305,000.

The data does not show the real picture regarding the number of new startups in the UK, as this data is restricted to those businesses which have decided to incorporate (Chapter 3). There will have been hundreds of thousands of other startups in 2013 to 2016 that didn't consider it appropriate to incorporate.

Further, the figures show that new company registrations are growing at a startling pace right across the UK, with Central London showing incorporations of 500 per

Table 1.1   UK Business Incorporations

Year	New Incorporated Businesses
2016	658,000
2015	608,000
2014	581,000
2013	527,000

1000 residents. The particular reason (the gig economy) behind this high level of incorporations will be discussed in detail in Chapter 5.

Interestingly, information from the Official Records Office in the UK also shows that there has recently been a decrease in the number of businesses failing, with a 4% reduction in company liquidations.

These healthy figures are not impressive, though, when compared with those coming from the USA where 543,000 new businesses are being set up each month. The UK figures are encouraging, however, given the political upheavals (such as Brexit) that have taken place in the last few years.

What are the reasons for the increased activity in new startups?

There has been a move by governments to outsource a number of their services to subcontractor businesses as part of cost-saving exercises. (We will look at the growth in subcontracting in detail in Chapter 5.)

These arrangements can often result in the governments in question circumventing their own employment legislation and avoiding expensive commitments (which can then become the problem of the subcontractor businesses!).

Another reason for the increase in the number of new startups is the number of graduates leaving education looking for a career, and on finding that there are few opportunities available decide to set up their own business.

It is also very easy to set up an online business from home, and relatively easy to obtain finance.

Government Assistance for New Businesses

At the moment, there is a lot of political will to encourage more new startup businesses, with grant funding, subsidies, assistance raising finance, exemptions from statutory reporting and tax incentives available to those who are willing to take the plunge. So, there couldn't be a better time to start.

Assistance with financing means that it is less risky now than it has been to start a business, as governments in some cases will underwrite startup loans.

Businesses can now be set up and registered in a matter of hours, as regulations have been relaxed.

I would advise that you take advice from a qualified business adviser in the area you are considering your startup, as to the assistance currently available locally. There is also a lot of advice available free online, but be wary of who you are taking advice from as there are plenty of rogues purporting to be more able than they are.

Governments have cottoned on to the fact that today's new startup businesses become tomorrow's major employers and taxpayers and have realized that by taking an active role in the creation of new business, they are ensuring a thriving future economy. Often, their involvement is not purely altruistic, as they find they have to fix economies that they have broken with their own policies.

The following details from the US Small Business Administration show how key small new startup businesses are to the economy. They define small businesses as enterprises having fewer than 500 employees, and there are 28 million of these businesses in the USA.

These small businesses employ over 50% of the US working population (currently 120 million individuals).

Sixty-five percent of new jobs created in the USA since 1995 have been created by small businesses.

Fifty-two percent of US small businesses are home based, with the fastest-growing sector being freelance businesses.

Government support in the form of innovation vouchers that subsidize advice for startups, and Entrepreneurs Relief, which reduces tax for business owners looking to sell their businesses, has helped more people to set up their own business.

So, with the level of assistance available at the moment, this is a good time to start a business.

I have already referred to the fact that businesses are increasingly being founded by people in their twenties and thirties. Figures from the Companies House UK website show that in 2017 almost 400,000 companies in the UK were founded by someone born during or after 1982.

Success Stories

My intention in writing this book is to provide you with all the information that you will need to build a skill set to run a successful business. It is hoped that by reading this book, you don't become a loser.

I have tried to do this by focusing on the right and the wrong things to do. But first, to whet your appetite, I have included some interesting information on the formation of some of the world's leading businesses.

Out of Acorns Giant Oaks Grow

This section looks at how some household names found their feet. Take note that there was often no big plan, the businesses just took off. By the time you have read this book, you will be able to identify why these businesses thrived while others failed.

eBay and PayPal

In 1995, a computer programmer, Pierre Omidyar, started auctioning off his personal belongings on his personal website, AuctionWeb, as a personal project. However, when the amount of web traffic made it necessary to upgrade to a business

Internet account and his costs increased from $30 a month to $250, he had to start charging people fees to make ends meet.

Pierre needed to take on staff to deal with the task of managing the cash he was receiving. He had not planned on setting up a business, but things escalated and he built up a team that could handle the volume of work, and turned the phenomena into a business.

His business and the website are now known as eBay.

At about the same time that eBay was setting up, Max Levchin was setting up Confinity, a business producing security software for handheld devices. He did not achieve enormous success with that business model, and decided to focus instead on developing an electronic wallet.

He then found that people were using the electronic wallet as an eBay auction currency.

Max had not intended to work with eBay, but Confinity soon became consumed by that business.

Eventually, Confinity expanded its operations and changed its name to PayPal. Thereafter, it was taken over by eBay.

Pierre made himself and Max very rich by auctioning off his belongings!

Neither of them started out with the plan to run the businesses they ended up with!

Starbucks

Howard Schultz started his business the classic way, which is to work in a business long enough to know the ropes and then set up on your own.

Howard had worked for Starbucks, which at that time was a retailer of high-quality roasted coffee beans and not the chain of espresso coffee shops and cafes it is today.

It was on a trip to Milan that Howard saw the opportunity for a chain of upmarket espresso cafes, and he decided to leave Starbucks to set up 'Il Giornale', with funding provided by Starbucks, who saw his new venture as a potential customer for their roasted beans.

At that time, Starbucks had no interest in providing cafe facilities, so they were happy to help Howard. They also sold him their brand name.

From that inauspicious start in Seattle in 1987, Howard developed the business into the global brand we know today. This is a great example of knowing your business and doing it well.

Panasonic

Konosuke Matsushita, the founder of Panasonic, displayed a quality that is essential in the successful business owner, which is a strong belief in self and product.

In 1917, Konosuke, then a 23-year-old apprentice at an electrical company, invented an improved light socket, which his then employers had no interest in. He believed in the socket so much that he decided to leave his employment and concentrate on his invention.

He carried on improving it further until he had created a viable business, Matsushita Electric (which later became Panasonic).

Konosuke's belief in himself and his creative talent drove him to create products that other electrical businesses were not producing, such as battery-powered cycle lamps.

The key to Konosuke's success was his willingness to take a risk on his ability. He was confident enough to follow his belief that his product was as good as he thought it was.

Konksuke became one of Japan's richest men, but because of his humble beginnings he held a far from average view on business ethics. He believed that he should create wealth for all, as well as himself.

Konksuke believed that business should create wealth for society as a whole, as well as for shareholders, and he was a major contributor to charity.

Apple

Steve Wozniak had been working on the design of a small personal computer for a number of years, but hadn't got very far in creating a business until he met Steve Jobs, an old school friend. Steve Wozniak displayed the creativity and had the imagination to produce a world-beating product, but hadn't been able to exploit his position.

Steve Jobs instantly saw the commercial potential of Wozniak's work, and got to work on branding and selling the first Apple products.

The two Steves had been friends since high school. They had both dropped out of college and gained employment at Atari. It wasn't until Steve Wozniak displayed a phone router at a computer club, which both he and Steve Jobs attended, that their association began.

Steve Jobs convinced Steve Wozniak to join him in a business, which initially had no funding. However, he managed to convince their suppliers, who provided the parts to make the first batch of computers, that the proceeds of Apple's first sales would be enough to pay for their bills.

He did this with the assistance of his major customer, who verified the details with the suppliers. This was enough for Apple to fulfill its first big order, and the rest is history.

Steve Jobs had found a unique way to finance his soon-to-be multibillion-dollar company. That was in 1976.

When Apple went public in 1980, it generated more money than any public sale of a business since Ford Motor Company in 1956.

Between 1976 and 1980, Apple had difficulties raising finance because banks at the time did not think the idea of a computer for everybody made any sense. It wasn't until Mike Markkula, a professional business investor, underwrote a business loan of $250,000 for Apple, that the business was safe.

It is said that Steve Jobs visited Mike Markkula at his home to coax him out of retirement, to ensure that the deal went ahead.

Steve Jobs had the vision to see the world we live in today, and to see the advances in technology that allowed the development of products such as the iPhone.

Apple is an example of a collection of talented individuals coming together to make the perfect whole. It is also another example of someone with total confidence in themselves and their product.

The company has consistently increased its income since its formation, from sales of $773,000 in 1977 to sales of $215.6 billion in 2016.

These four examples tell the tale of some of our most successful business people and the lessons that can be learned from their success.

Chapter 2

So You Want to Run Your Own Business

Chapter 1 showed that a high level of confidence, a vision for the future and a belief that 'it'll work' are essential for a successful business. But equally essential is a firm base upon which to start. This can only be achieved if you have asked yourself the following questions about your business: why, what, where, when and who (in no particular order).

The answers to these questions, as you will see in the following sections, will form the foundation upon which you will build. The final and most important question is: How do I start? This will be the topic covered in Chapter 3.

Why Are You Setting Up a Business?

The reason why you are setting up a business will have a big influence on its structure.

As we have seen, some businesses just set themselves up, with the proprietors reacting quickly to events as they play out.

But, no matter how unplanned the businesses appear, the proprietors at some stage will have to decide to take things forward on a business footing.

This involves seriously looking at the finances and resources available, and whether the outcome fits in with life plans.

Often, the rewards that the unexpected business offers are too much to discount, as the following examples show.

Viagra

A good example of an unplanned business is that of Viagra (sildenafil citrate), which was originally developed as a drug for treating pulmonary hypertension and angina.

It was during Phase I of the drug's clinical trials that the unexpected side effects in male patients were observed. Pfizer, an existing commercial organization set up to bring new pharmaceuticals to market, decided to develop a significant separate business for Viagra for treating erectile dysfunction.

A chance discovery that secured almost $2 billion a year in net sales for Pfizer before the loss of exclusivity.

Evolution

Businesses have been known to evolve from a hobby or pastime (as happened to eBay – see Chapter 1) and are often driven by consumer demand for an underdeveloped product or service.

These days, social media can often be the driving force for such a startup, with the momentum of the enterprise outside the proprietor's control.

The power of social media takes over, and the growth in demand is fueled by online chat, such as Twitter.

The best way forward for such businesses in this position is to call a halt, take a breather and come up with a manageable plan to progress, before physical and monetary resources are stretched too far.

Unemployment

If unemployment occurs unexpectedly, and without the benefit of redundancy benefits, there is often the will to set up a business, but also the lack of capital with which to do so.

But if capital can be acquired to fund the setting up of a business, it is likely that this option will be taken. This would not only be for the income benefit, but also to regain some purpose in life, as it's difficult to accept a life of doing nothing.

Unemployment/redundancy can often evoke a feeling of victimhood, and if this can be utilized as a driving force with which to set up a business, it gives the business a head start. This emotion should be embraced by the new business owner.

Often, the business will be set up as an aggressive competitor to the one responsible for the redundancy, utilizing the skills of the ex-employees.

You Can Do It Better

There must have been times in your life when you've had to wait for your orders to be dealt with, or you have noticed particularly bad customer service and said to yourself that 'you could do better'. For most of us that would be the end of it, but there are entrepreneurs who see that as a business opportunity.

Or maybe you work for a business that is operating below par, and you think you could do better, as Howard Schultz did at Starbucks, where he identified a market that they had not considered.

If this is the position you find yourself in, you will have a better chance of successfully setting up a new business, as you have prior knowledge of the business sector, and you are not gambling on a new business in a new sector.

Often, people find themselves employed by businesses in which they have little respect, and they can get to the point where they do not want to be ordered about by someone who they think is lacking.

But only a few do anything about it and set up on their own. What makes them different from the rest? In a word, it's confidence. You should always have confidence in your decisions.

There is a thin line between confidence in an off-the-wall idea and delusion, especially when the rest of the world is against you. But, it is having the ability to identify if you're going off-plan and the ability to defeat your doubts that leads to success.

A Eureka Moment

The following are a couple of examples of businesses that started following a chance discovery, where the thought of a business development could not have been further from the mind, the doubters were ignored and a business was formed.

The Post-it Note

Dr. Spencer Silver, working for the Minnesota, Mining and Manufacturing Company (The 3M Company), invented a low-tack, pressure-sensitive adhesive, which for years went unacknowledged until Arthur Fry, one of his colleagues, had a eureka moment in church and came up with a practical use for it. Arthur Fry was fed up with his bookmarks falling from his hymnbook and applied Dr. Silver's adhesive to some paper to mark his pages.

Realizing what a practical item he had discovered, he ignored those with little enthusiasm for his idea and spent no time in letting the world in on his secret – the Post-it note.

He became engrossed in bringing the Post-it note to market, working tirelessly with Dr. Silver to do so.

The reason they are yellow is that they found some scrap yellow paper when they were working on the prototype.

This is another example of a business evolving with no plan.

Although this example is the accepted tale of the invention of the Post-it note, a Swiss inventor, Alan Amron, claims he invented them first, but offers very little evidence to back his claim.

His claims through the courts for his rights have been dismissed.

While talking of the Swiss…

Velcro

One day, George de Mestral, a Swiss engineer, took his dog for a walk in the woods. When he got back, he was annoyed by all the burrs stuck to his pants and how difficult it was to remove them. When he looked at the burrs under a micro-scope, he saw that they had tiny hooks that had attached themselves to the loops of thread in his pants.

George set about finding a practical use for this phenom-enon, and in 1955 he invented Velcro. He was convinced that he had a useful product, ignored his doubters and set up a company to refine his product and bring it to market. The Velcro companies are still trading to this day.

Technological Developments

There are still endless possibilities for new businesses as the 21st century has brought with it a number of challenges and opportunities. There are opportunities to develop new and cleaner sources of power, make our cities more sustainable and improve our communities with the latest technological developments.

Every technological advancement brings with it the death of old industries, and opportunities for new ones. The progress that is being made on personal transportation and the development of drones will lead to major changes in society, along with opportunities for new markets to open up.

You should look around and try to spot issues that are going to affect you and those in your community. When advances such as driverless cars become generally accepted, is there an opportunity for creating a remote taxi system?

Singapore has already started a trial of autonomous taxis, and driverless buses are already operating in Helsinki and Lyon.

Tesla boss Elon Musk believes that a fully autonomous car for general use is only 2 years away.

Plans for an autonomous car sharing company have already been mooted, where, rather than cars spending most their lives parked up and idle, they are shared.

Given the time and space devoted to parking cars, this is a valid concept.

Developing an Idea

Once you have identified a business opportunity, you need to develop a business plan. Plenty of agencies have been set up to provide assistance to potential new businesses, with drafting business plans as their main aim. Often, these agencies are government sponsored as part of their business initiative schemes.

A business plan turns an idea into a viable business, with revenues and expenses identified and forecast. Drafting a business plan will be dealt with in detail in Chapter 3.

Many business startups fail because the 'idea' was never formulated into a viable business plan. A business needs to generate income and earn a profit, and these basic requirements should not be overlooked.

Many failed businesses often concentrate more on publicizing their idea than they do on the income streams that they can produce.

Vanity

If you are motivated by the idea of a fleet of wagons with your name on them, or your own Trump Towers, you will need to ask yourself if displaying your success is a valid basis upon which to build a business.

There are a few individuals with the talent, and often the funding, to make anything a success and they can set up numerous businesses for themselves and their families, to display their ability and wealth to the world.

If you are not lucky enough to be one of the talented few, may I remind you that the level of work necessary to make a business a success is high, as is the failure rate of new businesses.

(On this note, if you are tempted to display your newfound wealth, should your business succeed, by purchasing fancy cars and a big house, forget it. You will regret every pound you spend when, in your retirement, you calculate the amount of money you wasted. I say this from experience, as a previous owner of Range Rovers and Porsches. You don't need to impress the people who matter.)

You Want to Be Rich

There is nothing wrong with dreaming that you can run your own business and become rich in the process, but there is a lot of hard work involved and many sacrifices to be made.

You need to decide whether you want to be a billionaire and incur all the penalties that will entail. Do you want the business to run you and risk losing family and friends, or do you want to control the demands that the business will make on you?

You will need to consider whether you will ever let the business run you, or will you run the business (and remember this decision when customer demands are encroaching on family commitments).

Identify at an early stage the level of income you will need to provide a good lifestyle for you and your family.

Once you establish the reason why you want to set up a business, you need to answer the other questions.

What Is Your Business Going to Do?

This may seem like a strange question, but many potential startups have failed due to their creators not being able to turn their ideas into a workable business format. This has become common in the digital age, where ideas for a radical website can be dashed when the costings are considered.

There are many new business formats that would not have been conceived a generation ago, such as Spotify with its music streaming services. There are also many occupations that had never been thought of when I was receiving careers advice.

Don't be scared to be the first to do something new. Start with a blank sheet and invent something.

There must be a positive cash flow; you need to be producing something that people are willing to pay for, be it customers, or possibly, advertisers (willing to fund your YouTube or Twitter page).

Too many people are giving things away online and spending fruitless hours on projects that will never produce any income.

We have already seen that businesses can end up doing things far different from their intended purpose.

Unique Selling Point

With regard to 'what the business is going to do', many businesses look for a unique selling point (USP) that will distinguish them from the competition, and they look for novel or new ways to provide the services they offer.

The USP can be seen as a factor that differentiates a business from its competitors, such as the lowest cost, the highest quality or the first-ever product of its kind. It can simply be thought of as what you have and your competitors don't.

You can find reliance upon USPs in the catering sector where businesses concentrate more on the experience they provide than the product they sell.

The idea is that the memorable experience will distinguish them from their competitors and generate customer loyalty.

Interestingly, the product does not need to be different from that of the competitors. If a business is successful in its marketing, at pointing out some benefits of a product being sold that the competitors have not picked up on, that business will sell more of that product.

Making a product more expensive can give it a perceived superiority in the marketplace.

Where Should You Set Your Business Up (Both Virtually and Actually)?

Could your new business be run on a shoestring from home, will it need a retail outlet or will it need a purpose-built facility? The answer to these questions will have an impact on the finances needed to get the project off the ground.

If you are considering starting a retail business, the position of the operation can be of prime importance. The old adage 'location, location, location' still applies today, and I would advise that substantial research is undertaken into the location of the business. This will pay dividends, even if it means actually 'staking out' a spot and counting the footfall.

Don't try and re-invent the wheel when considering a location; use your competitors' research efforts and ask yourself why they chose that location. Watch how many customers visit their premises and establish if any benefits could be gained by locating nearby.

Bear in mind your customers' traveling and existing shopping habits and consider how much they would need to alter those habits to use your business.

This advice applies to a physical presence, and a similar approach is needed for the virtual world. Your web designer is key to your online presence, and your use of social media will be important in attracting traffic to your website (there is further advice regarding Internet presence in Chapter 8).

Online businesses can be operated from anywhere, as long as local laws allow you to trade accordingly.

See Chapter 7 for further details regarding the location of a business.

When Should You Start Your Business?

You shouldn't start your business until you have everything ready, and enough resources to deal with initial demand. Many businesses have raced to market, trying to beat their potential competitors, but have failed as they haven't had the resources to meet demand.

There is also an ideal time to bring a business to market, which is sometimes governed by external factors. YouTube, for example, was released in 2005 and was an immediate success. If someone had tried to set up a similar business some years earlier, before there was the ubiquitous wireless Internet and video cameras in most phones, it might not have been such a hit.

Ensure that you have done all your marketing and have people waiting at your door the morning you start.

My advice is that you don't start until you have double-checked your tick list that everything is in place and all eventualities catered for.

Who Should You Go into Business With?

Lots of good friendships and marriages have been ruined by ill-conceived business partnerships. They have been the cause of many a family rift too; the Dassler brothers being the most famous dispute, which led to rivalry between two of the world's most recognizable brands.

The Dasslers

In the 1920s, two brothers were partners in the Dassler Brothers Sports Shoe Company. Adolf (Adi) and Rudolph (Rudi) Dassler complimented each other; Adi was the designer and craftsman, while Rudolph was a natural salesman.

Due to family tensions they fell out (allegedly their wives fell out), and while Rudi was on active service and subsequently a prisoner of war during the Second World War, Adi was left to run the business, which he did with much success, and prospered.

Rudi resented Adi being left with the business, and his own lack of prosperity. He blamed his call-up and capture on Adi, and a conflict ensued between the brothers.

The conflict escalated dramatically, and the brothers split the business in two in 1948, dividing the assets and the employees between them.

Adi named his company 'Adidas', a combination of his first and last names. Rudi attempted the same by first naming his company 'Ruda' but eventually changing it to 'Puma'.

The conflict grew, with the town where the brothers' factories were located taking sides in the dispute. Local businesses served only one brother or the other and dating or marrying across company lines was forbidden.

The negative cost of this dispute was that while they were focused on each other, they were unable to react to Nike, who began to dominate the market they were in.

Work as a Team

A common reason for disputes in businesses is where the key employees don't think that they are getting adequately remunerated. This is common in the catering trade, where an individual sets up a restaurant or eating establishment, which becomes very popular, and often the chef is an employee.

When the chef realizes that the success of the business is mainly due to his/her culinary skills, he/she requests a share of the profits. This request is often a cause of friction between the proprietor and the chef, and in a number of cases results in the cessation of the business.

This can happen in all types of business, so the lesson to learn is that the business should work as a team, and the profits should be shared with those who have a significant role in generating them.

When you realize that it can't be done on your own, and you need to collaborate as a team, you will get more from the staff as they are more motivated to make it work.

You really do need to consider carefully before you try to do it on your own or take a partner on!

You will see in Chapter 3 that a number of business models do allow for the sharing of the business profits, and the options are endless.

So, if you decide at this stage that the business is going to be operated by a number of individuals, the format to allow for this can be finalized later.

The format for JT's Restaurant (a fictional business startup that we will refer to throughout the book) is interesting, as the proprietors decide to take their agreed shares in completely different ways.

JT's Restaurant is operated by an entrepreneur (myself!) as a sole trader, employing a chef on an agreed (generous) salary. The reason for this setup is due to various factors that are explained in Chapter 12.

(Further details regarding JT's Restaurant can be found in the section 'Example of Business Plan/Finance Application' in Chapter 12.)

What Should You Call Your Business?

This is one of the most important decisions you will make about the startup, as the name will identify the business. It is important, therefore, that the name identifies what you do, and that it is a name you can live with for a while.

Search engines and the like need to be considered when deciding on the name, because if you want your site to appear first, you will need a name higher up the alphabet. Many businesses do this by including a number of A's before the major business name. You will need to think about how your customers would view this approach before using it! It is popular with taxi firms wanting their telephone number to be ahead of their competitors in the phone listings.

Also bear in mind what it will look like as an Internet address. Pen Island didn't realize that their Internet address would read as penisland.net, and Speed of Art didn't realize that their online presence could be misconstrued as a site for Speedo wearers with wind problems.

You should check on the company registers that someone else hasn't already taken the name you have chosen; another way is to Google the name and see what comes up.

If you decide to use a name in another language, you will need to check what it means first. Powergenitalia.com is an Italian power company that needs advice on its company name.

Keep the name short and think about a logo and branding at the same time. Think of the image that the name will portray.

It is possible to change the name at a future date, but you may lose confused customers and incur additional expense in printing costs, redesigning your website, etc. So, it is important to get it right first time.

I have been director of companies called Cooking the Books Limited and The Money Laundry Limited, both of which traded within the law, I may add.

A sense of humor is allowed when considering a name.

Going through the thought processes and asking yourself the foregoing questions will help enormously when undertaking your initial business plan.

If, after reading this chapter, you decide that you are not ready to start your own business from scratch, you could always buy an existing business that may be for sale. This option is explored in Chapter 4.

Chapter 3

How Do You Start?

The Business Plan

You don't need a degree in business studies to run a success-ful business, but you do need to know some basic economics (you sell and your customer buys).

You also need a modicum of common sense, which is often sadly lacking in those who fail in their attempts to run a business.

The first stage in setting up a business is to draft a business plan, which will identify whether the business will generate a profit and provide a living wage for yourself.

It is important that this task is undertaken first, because if the business does not look like a goer at this stage, it will be a waste of time devoting any further effort to it.

The drafting of a business plan is so key to the creation of a successful business that I have run through the process and included a plan for a hypothetical restaurant (JT's Restaurant) in Chapter 12.

The plan covers the period from startup until the third year of trading and deals with all aspects of the business startup.

The creation of a business plan is one of the most impor-tant steps to take as it serves as a road map for the early years of the business. It also outlines the route that the business will take to reach its annual and revenue targets.

Drafting a business plan may involve you revisiting some of the questions dealt with in previous chapters.

There are lots of organizations and resources available to small businesses to help with their business plans.

The detail required to draft a business plan becomes apparent in the budgeting and cash flow section in this chapter.

Create a Brand, Logo and Business Design

You need to create a brand, logo and business design so that your customers can find you and your products. I would advise that you start with a blank sheet of paper and think of designs that fit with the business that you are going to operate.

I would also advise that your slogan, if you have one, is clearly understood. One that was misunderstood, to great benefit, is Nike's 'Just do it', which a young Indian man mistook to mean Just do IT (information technology). He went on to form one of India's major IT companies.

Next, look at brands that you like and see if you can come up with one of your own that is similar, but not so similar that it could be construed as a copy.

Don't restrict yourself to one design, but come up with a few along a theme, and fine-tune them on your basic software before you hand your initial thoughts over to a professional graphic designer.

Rethink about how your company name will fit with the brand and logo and remember that nothing is set in stone at this stage.

I would advise that you appoint a professional graphic designer to produce the final design, as you will get something that looks professional.

Remember that your customers will associate the brand and logo with you, and if it looks like it's done on a shoestring they will associate that approach with your business. If it looks cheap, your customers will think you are too.

The graphic designer should be able to advise on the use of colors, how to avoid those that will clash and how your brand will look online and on letterheads. Keep it simple.

Keep an eye out for bad design in others and learn from their mistakes.

Some suggest that you should restrict your brand design to four colors plus black and white, so that it is easy to replicate.

Once you've agreed on a design, you can produce what is known as a brand guideline, which typically includes:

■ A copy of the logo
■ An inversion of the logo (black on white/white on black)
■ Your agreed colors
■ Typeface

This design can be adopted on all the business stationary (whether online or actually printed). This guideline is an important document as it will include all the color codes and design parameters to give to printers in the future, as the business develops (i.e., business cards for new employees).

As I am not an artist, nor have I any intention to be one, I have made no effort at this stage to include a design for the sake of this book.

Sole Trader, Limited Company or Partnership?

Now that you have branded your name, you next need to decide which business format you are going to adopt to run your business.

The decision as to which format the business adopts upon setup is dependent upon whether a number of people are involved in the business. If you are planning to run the business on your own and employ anyone you need assistance from, then the sole trader format is for you.

Sole Trader

This ensures that you solely will benefit from the business's success (unless you decide to pay bonuses to the staff from the profits made).

The sole trader approach is flexible, and arrangements can be made to minimize the tax paid and to maximize the proprietor's pension/retirement plans. You will need to speak to tax advisers in your location as to the options available.

For various reasons (which are apparent in the business plan/finance application in Chapter 12) it has been agreed that JT's Restaurant be set up as a sole trader format.

A sole trader business is the quickest to set up as there is very little paperwork or formalities. The Tax Authorities only need to be told that you have started running a business. In the UK, this needs to be done by 5 October in your second tax year of trading (I would advise that you take professional advice on this and register as soon as possible so that you do not build up liabilities to tax and national insurance).

The main disadvantage of the sole trader approach is that you are solely liable for the debts of the business should it be unable to clear its liabilities.

Another disadvantage to being a sole trader is that you need to enter into contracts with your employees personally, which means that you will need to pay their salaries even if the business income is nil; in that situation, this could mean that you may be the only one not getting paid!

(You can possibly get round this by offering zero-hours contracts to the staff, which means that as an employer you are not obliged to guarantee any fixed working hours or salaries. Zero-hours contracts are very popular in the 'gig' economy we have today, but the morality of utilizing them is questionable [more on this in Chapter 5].)

From a tax and legal perspective, if you are a sole trader, you are treated as earning the income personally and all the assets and liabilities of the business are in your personal name.

In the hypothetical business, JT's Restaurant, all the liabilities will be mine, as the business has been set up as a sole trader. But given that my involvement is solely to provide security, and I have faith in the business, it is not something that I am worried about.

If the business is not financially sound or there are risks involved, it may be preferable to incorporate to gain the benefits of limited liability.

Limited Company (Incorporation)

This involves forming a limited liability company, which is a separate legal entity, so that the ownership of assets and the responsibility for debts are not yours, but they stay with the company.

Other than providing security, another major advantage of incorporation is taxation, as the rates of tax and the opportunities to reduce the amount of tax payable are better when a company is used to run the business.

If a business owner transfers his/her business to a limited company that they control, it can be treated as a sale for tax purposes (and a capital taxes liability may arise as a consequence).

If the company has just been set up to take over the business and it is unable to obtain funding, it will not have any cash to pay the business owner. The amount can remain unpaid and a director's loan (i.e., the company owes the amount to the director) can be set up to account for the amount due.

This amount can be withdrawn over a period of years as a small income to minimize the tax due on it.

From the foregoing information, you can see the opportunity to reduce tax through incorporation, and I would recommend that specialist advice is sought when a business is incorporated.

There are plenty of agents around who can form a company on your behalf, and I would advise that you take this route to ensure that you are compliant with corporate legislation.

When a company is formed, its ownership is determined by the holders of its shares. A company can have as many or as few shares as the business owner decides, but the more shares there are, the more compliance work there is to do.

The system of share ownership provides the opportunity for the business to be shared, that is, 2 shareholders could hold 50% of the shares each, or 10 shareholders could hold 10% each.

As you can see, using the company format provides opportunities to share the ownership of the business, and this can prove useful when deciding upon sharing the profits of the business.

But beware, each holder of a share in a company gets a vote in the running of the business, which is why a large number of business proprietors ensure that they, and their families, always retain more than 50% of the shares. This ensures that they always have control of the company.

The ownership of shares by the proprietor and his family further provides the opportunity to reduce tax by taking profits from the business by way of dividends.

Dividends are payments of a share of the profits from the company to the shareholders.

The payment of dividends has formed the basis of a number of tax saving schemes, whereby a spouse and children receive high levels of dividends, while the proprietor takes a low salary as earnings (more on this in Chapter 6).

The tax treatment of dividends and earnings is different, and this difference is exploited in tax saving schemes.

An example of a tax savings scheme utilizing dividends is provided in Chapter 6.

Incorporation is a complex legal process and advice needs to be taken if it is being considered.

As with all things, there is a catch. It costs more to operate a company as the accounts are more detailed and the company needs to comply with separate tax rules.

Partnerships

For those businesses where more than one person is involved, and the limited company option is deemed to be too complex or expensive, there is the option of partnership.

Partnerships offer the following advantages:

1. Economies of scale can be achieved by working with others, whether it is the ability to jointly purchase a property or the sharing of running costs.
2. Business owners working together can split the management role and assist each other in running the business.
3. A larger business can provide a broader selection of services.
4. A larger business can often attract better staff, and they can assist in the role of succession and ultimately the sale of the business.
5. Customers get more comfort dealing with a larger business as they feel that their consumer rights are more likely to be addressed.

Three basic formats of partnership are available:

■ Basic partnership
■ Expense sharing partnership
■ Limited liability partnership

The *basic partnership* is very much like the sole trader format of running a business, the only main issue remaining is that of unlimited liability. All partners will be liable for the faults/mistakes of all the other partners, so unless you have full trust in your partners this may not be the best option for you.

In a basic partnership, the partners share profits in an agreed profit sharing ratio with their income and expenses being allocated accordingly.

In these businesses, a single set of accounts is usually prepared, which will show the partners' individual profit shares and their capital investment in the business.

The basic partnership is required to submit a partnership tax return disclosing each partner's profit share to the Tax Authorities.

An *expense sharing partnership* is very much like a normal partnership, but specific streams of income and expenditure are allocated to specific partners. There is still unlimited liability.

Professional practices, for example dentists, often adopt this business model, where they tend to share the costs of the property overheads, but account for individual income and incur separate specific costs related to their individual patients.

Expense sharing partnerships are treated differently for taxation and accounting purposes, as each partner can provide different services and work different hours from the others.

Each partner will draft their own accounts and will submit an individual tax return each year; normally, a partnership return is not submitted.

Expense sharing partnerships are common where it is easy to identify individual partners' income and the expense relating to each partner, for example the costs of running separate buildings and specific staff or the cost of running certain fixtures and equipment.

The unlimited liability issue can be dealt with by forming a *limited liability partnership*. This can be incorporated without any shareholders. What is needed, however, is a detailed partnership agreement, which provides the legal framework that stipulates the duties and general conduct of the company members (partners).

The legal and taxation rules which apply to limited liability partnerships vary and can be more complex than those applicable to normal partnerships.

The partnership agreement of a limited liability partnership has a number of key areas which are mandatory. I would advise any partnership, be it limited liability or unincorporated, to have a detailed agreement to provide for any future disputes.

The core of any partnership is trust between the partners, knowing that each partner has the ability and will work to the best of their ability, for the benefit of the partnership.

Most good commercial lawyers should be able to provide an adequate partnership agreement, as they should have one in place in their own practice.

Budgeting and Cash Flow

Now that you have sorted out your name and business format, it's time to look at whether you're going to make any money.

As you are setting up the business to earn an income, you should know enough about the finances of your business to be able to produce some kind of budget or forecast before you start. The drafting of a forecast should be the first thing you do, primarily to ascertain whether you are going to make any money!

It is relatively straightforward to do this and numerous computer programs are available which allow businesses to produce detailed financial projections.

It is unlikely that a business will generate sufficient income to cover the business expenditure from day one. It may be a while before the business is generating enough money to match or exceed expenditure, and it is necessary to plan for this deficit upon set up.

The funds to cover the shortfall may need to be borrowed, and in order to convince the lender that the need for their financial support is not open-ended, it is necessary to show them when the business can afford to begin paying them back.

Ultimately, the business will be set up to provide the proprietor with a living, and it is essential to determine when the business will be able to afford to do this.

Bankers are more keen to lend to businesses that work to budgets and prepare financial forecasts.

A projection is useful to deal with the foregoing points, and a by-product of producing forecasts of expenses is that the first sales targets of the business are set.

Figures 3.1 through 3.3 provide a simple example of a cash flow that reflects the first 3 years of JT's Restaurant business.

The figures are based on a cash flow produced for an actual startup restaurant I advised.

The schedules have been produced by a computer program called Excel, which is a market leader in the production of cash flows and is relatively easy to use.

The figures in Figure 3.1 show that the restaurant produces a cash flow deficit of £841 in its first year, but then goes on to produce excesses of £22,999 in the second year and £36,689 in the third year (Figures 3.2 and 3.3).

The figures show that the business needs an overdraft of £19,999 in March in the first year, but goes on to generate a cash balance of £58,846 at the end of the 3-year period.

The figures, which I have hijacked for my hypothetical JT's Restaurant, include an annual salary of £60,000 for the chef as well as the drawings figure, which when added to the final cash balance of £58,846, give a very healthy return from the business.

The combined income figures over the 3-year period drawn by the business team are as follows:

Chef's salary £60,000 for 3 years	£180,000
Proprietor's drawings	£74,400

In addition, £58,846 is available for the proprietor to draw (ignoring the tax costs at this stage).

At this stage, it looks as though the proprietor has gained less from the business than the chef, but the business will have built up a capital value in the period, which would belong solely to the proprietor.

Receipts	July	August	September	October	November	December	January	February	March	April	May	June	Total
Sales													
Total	44235	53090	39810	35380	22140	26565	8855	17710	22140	39810	39810	35380	384925
Expenses													
Purchases	17695	19855	14135	11110	6865	7440	4430	5490	5935	10630	10630	10260	124475
Staff wages	12000	12000	12000	12000	10000	10000	10000	12000	12000	12000	12000	12000	138000
Rates	650	650	650	650	650	650	650	650	650	650	650	650	7800
Rent	2000	2000	2000	2000	2000	2000	2000	2000	2000	2000	2000	2000	24000
Water rates	175			175			175			175			1400
Heat and light	800	800	800	800	800	800	800	800	800	800	800	800	9600
Insurance	900						900						1800
Advertising	200				200		200						600
Printing and stationery	200												200
Telephone			450			450			450			450	1800
Repairs	1000						1500						2500
Legal fees	1000												1000
Accountancy	250	250	250	250	250	250	250	250	250	250	250	250	3000
Sundry expenses	100	100	100	100	100	100	100	100	100	100	100	100	1200
Credit card charges	50	50	50	50	50	50	50	50	50	50	50	50	600
Bank charges	100	100	100	100	100	100	100	100	100	100	100	100	1200
Loan repayments	849	849	849	849	849	849	849	849	849	849	849	849	10191
VAT payment			11500			7500			7500			7500	34000
Drawings	1700	1700	1700	1700	1700	1700	1700	1700	1700	1700	1700	1700	20400
Set up costs -	2000												2000
													0
Total costs	41669	38354	44584	29784	23564	31889	23704	23989	32384	29304	29129	37409	385766
Surplus/(deficit)	2566	14736	−4774	5596	−1424	−5324	−14849	−6279	−10244	10506	10681	−2029	−841
Cumulative bank balance	2566	17301	12527	18123	16699	11374	−3475	−9754	−19999	−9493	1188	−841	

Figure 3.1 JT's Restaurant 3-year forecast: Year 1.

Receipts	July	August	September	October	November	December	January	February	March	April	May	June	Total
Sales													
Total	48655	58400	43790	38920	24355	29220	9740	19480	24350	43790	43790	38920	423410
Expenses													
Purchases	19465	21840	15550	12220	7550	8185	4875	6040	6530	11690	11690	11285	136920
Staff wages	12700	12700	12700	12700	10500	10500	10500	10500	12700	12700	12700	12700	143600
Rates	650	650	650	650	650	650	650	650	650	650	650	650	7800
Rent	2000	2000	2000	2000	2000	2000	2000	2000	2000	2000	2000	2000	24000
Water rates	175			175			175			175		700	1400
Heat and light	800	800	800	800	800	800	800	800	800	800	800	800	9600
Insurance	900						900						1800
Advertising	200			200			200						600
Printing and stationery	200												200
Telephone			450			450			450			450	1800
Repairs	1000					1500							2500
Accountancy	250	250	250	250	250	250	250	250	250	250	250	250	3000
Sundry expenses	100	100	100	100	100	100	100	100	100	100	100	100	1200
Credit card charges	50	50	50	50	50	50	50	50	50	50	50	50	600
Bank charges	100	100	100	100	100	100	100	100	100	100	100	100	1200
Loan repayments	849	849	849	849	849	849	849	849	849	849	849	849	10191
VAT payment			7500			7500			7500			7500	30000
Drawings	2000	2000	2000	2000	2000	2000	2000	2000	2000	2000	2000	2000	24000
Total costs	41439	41339	42999	31894	25049	33434	24949	23339	33979	31364	31189	39434	400411
Surplus/(deficit)	7216	17061	791	7026	-694	-4214	-15209	-3859	-9629	12426	12601	-514	22999
B/f	-841												
Cumulative bank balance	6374	23435	24226	31251	30557	26343	11133	7274	-2355	10071	22671	22157	

Figure 3.2 JT's Restaurant 3-year forecast: Year 2.

Receipts	July	August	September	October	November	December	January	February	March	April	May	June	Total
Sales													
Total	53520	64240	48169	42812	26790	32142	10714	21428	26785	48169	48169	42812	465750
Expenses													
Purchases	21415	24025	17105	13445	8305	9005	5365	6645	7185	12860	12860	12415	150630
Staff wages	13470	13470	13470	13470	11050	11050	11050	11050	11050	13470	13470	13470	149540
Rates	650	650	650	650	650	650	650	650	650	650	650	650	7800
Rent	2000	2000	2000	2000	2000	2000	2000	2000	2000	2000	2000	2000	24000
Water rates	175		175	175			175			175		700	1400
Heat and light	800	800	800	800	800	800	800	800	800	800	800	800	9600
Insurance	900						900						1800
Advertising	200				200		200						600
Printing and stationery	200												200
Telephone			450			450			450			450	1800
Repairs	1000						1500						2500
Accountancy	250	250	250	250	250	250	250	250	250	250	250	250	3000
Sundry expenses	100	100	100	100	100	100	100	100	100	100	100	100	1200
Credit card charges	50	50	50	50	50	50	50	50	50	50	50	50	600
Bank charges	100	100	100	100	100	100	100	100	100	100	100	100	1200
Loan repayments	849	849	849	849	849	849	849	849	849	849	849	849	10191
VAT payment			8250			8250			8250			8250	33000
Drawings	2500	2500	2500	2500	2500	2500	2500	2500	2500	2500	2500	2500	30000
Total costs	44659	44794	46574	34389	26854	36054	26489	24994	34234	33804	33629	42584	429061
Surplus/(deficit)	8861	19446	1595	8423	-64	-3912	-15775	-3566	-7449	14365	14540	228	36689
B/f	22157												
Cumulative bank balance	31018	50463	52058	60481	60417	56504	40729	37163	29713	44078	58618	58846	

Figure 3.3 JT's Restaurant 3-year forecast: Year 3.

The business which was the inspiration for these figures never went ahead; the chef took a position catering for billionaires on a superyacht.

Financial forecasts form the basis of any business plan and are key in obtaining any finance that is needed. In this instance, the forecasts were shown to a bank manager, and a loan to purchase the business and an overdraft of £20,000 were requested.

The estimates of income and expenses in these forecasts were based on the experience of the chef, and expenses and margins generated by similar businesses.

Forecasts should be reviewed against the actual bank balance each month and any significant differences investigated, as this is what the bank manager will be doing in order to deal with any problems before they happen.

A good bank manager will ring you up when he thinks things are going awry, which is better than you trying to build up the nerve to go and tell him that things aren't going to plan.

By working to financial forecasts, you can pick up problems early and do something about them before they bring the business down. Often, the bank manager, with his experience, can identify the business's problems and provide solutions.

If income isn't as high as expected, you can concentrate your efforts on attracting further custom, and if you're spending too much you can introduce a period of austerity. Achieving the figures in the forecast is key to the success of the business.

A financial forecast should include room for maneuver should things not go to plan, in this case it is the drawings figure (the amount that I am proposing to take from the business).

A proprietor would normally reduce his income to make up for any shortfall in the forecasted profits, because if the business is not making money, where is the income for drawings going to come from?

Although the final figure (£58,846) from the previous example looks healthy, what is not included in the forecasts is the tax that is payable on the profits (at least the cash is still there to pay it!).

Tax can be quite significant, and even at a basic rate, as in the previous example, would account for at least £11,769. This would be in addition to the tax that the chef would need to pay on his £60,000 salary over the 3 years.

A business plan would normally include further details as to how the figures on the forecasts have been calculated, and, ideally, I would have liked to include further details of the figures on these cash flows in the business plan, which can be found in the section 'Example of a Business Plan/Finance Application' in Chapter 12.

The foregoing sales and purchases figures have been based on those achieved by the existing business operating from the premises, but they have been adjusted for inflation-ary factors.

The staff wages were calculated by the chef, based on the number of staff he thought he would need to run the busi-ness successfully.

All the other figures are based on historic values, adjusted by the chef for his specific circumstances; they are educated estimates and not pure guesswork.

I don't need to overstate that the accuracy of forecasts is key to the business's success as the confidence of lenders can be affected by shortfalls in achieving targets.

It is fundamental for a business to work to financial targets. If you work to targets and monitor your progress (I would suggest monthly), you will have more of a feel for how your business is performing and will not have any nasty surprises.

Pricing and Costings

How much should you sell your product/service for? If you are the only one providing the service and you have no competi-tion, you can set the price as high as you think you can get away with.

Pharmaceutical companies are very good at this; when they bring new drugs to market, they take the opportunity to recoup their substantial research costs by making huge profits on their products while they are still under license.

Interestingly, they can charge more for animal products than they can those used to deal with human medical conditions.

If you haven't got the luxury of being able to charge what you want, you will have to refer to your costs to ensure that they are being covered, when you calculate your sales price.

While setting your prices, you need to bear in mind the costs that need to be covered by your income.

In the example of JT's Restaurant, the price of the dishes needs to be enough to cover the cost of the food, the wages and all the overheads, not to mention a little extra to provide a profit for drawings.

In this case, multiplying the cost of the food by two and a half to three times provides sufficient income to cover the costs and provide an income.

Once the chef identifies the prices that he wants to charge, he then needs to compare the amounts with those that his competitors are charging for similar dishes.

You always need to take your competitors' prices into account when calculating your own, as your customers will.

If you think that you are supplying a premium product, and you think that your customers will be willing to pay extra for it, you will be justified in charging a premium.

Interestingly, customers often perceive that by paying a premium they are getting a better product.

However, consumers are getting wise to the fact that expensive does not always mean better. This has proved true with the success of discount retailers who have taken on premium brands with their own cut-price alternatives.

Conversely, for a number of years the major supermarkets worked on the basis that 'the perception of being cheaper is more important than actually being cheaper', by advertising that their products were the cheapest that the consumer could buy, when in fact they weren't.

Again, the rise in popularity of the discount retailers is indicative that this approach is no longer viable, as consumers can now see through the supermarkets' deception regarding sales prices.

The lesson that the supermarkets have learned is that the customer is no longer interested in loyalty bonuses or premium products but prefers to get the best product for the cheapest price.

This lesson should not be ignored by the new business owner.

The cut-price airlines initially set up with this premise in mind; however, as time has gone on, in order to maximize the return to shareholders, they have initiated practices to raise prices, which have taken them away from their low-price deals.

We will look at these practices and other methods of maximizing profitability in Chapter 9.

Chapter 4

Buying and Selling a Business

In this chapter, we will look at the issues that can arise upon the purchase or sale of a business and highlight the common pitfalls that may occur in the process.

We will look at the transaction from both the buyers' and the sellers' viewpoint and note the conflicts that may arise between the two.

The impact the transaction will have upon the business owner's taxation position will be outlined only briefly at this stage, with further detail provided in Chapter 6, when taxation will be looked at in detail.

Rather than setting up a business from scratch, there is always the option of buying an existing business that is up for sale. As this will provide an income from the date of takeover, it is a better option to look at if there is one available in the business sector within which you have experience.

JT's forecasts (Chapter 3) are based on the chef taking over an existing restaurant, a business that he has personal knowledge of and is confident will produce a good income.

The business that is to become JT's Restaurant is priced at £120,000, £60,000 of which is to be borrowed from a bank, hence the monthly loan repayments of £849 in the financial forecast.

For the purpose of the cash flow, the loan interest is calculated based on the loan being a repayment loan over a 10-year period at the rate of 11.65%.

The interest rate reflects the fact that the loan is mainly to finance goodwill (more on this in Chapter 7) and that the restaurant property is not available to secure the loan on (see further details of the finance application in Chapter 12).

As a rule, lenders tend to charge a higher interest rate on loans when they have little tangible security. In the example of JT's Restaurant, as the setup is far from straightforward and Tony (the chef) has a bad credit rating, the lender chooses to charge a higher rate.

However, from the forecasts, as the loan repayments are affordable, the lender's offer has been accepted.

No offer of finance should be turned down out of hand, as another may not be forthcoming. What is important is whether the business can afford the repayments.

Conversely, it's no use saddling a business with an unaffordable repayment liability if the effect on the cash flow is likely to bring the business down.

If normal channels of financing do not prove successful, it may be worth looking at the alternatives (see section 'Crowdfunding').

From the vendor's (seller's) point of view, it is very important that any confidential information regarding the business is withheld until the transfer of the business is fairly advanced.

If the existing staff become aware of a transfer of the business, they may voice their concerns and have fears for their employment status. It may be unsettling for them and could have an impact on the business.

It is likely that the structure of the business sale will be governed by tax legislation. The purchaser will usually be more relaxed regarding the tax treatment of the purchase than the vendor is regarding the sale.

The reason for this is that the purchaser's additional tax costs relating to the structure of the sale may not be payable upon their sale of the business many years in the future.

Is the Price Right?

If you are buying an existing business, the retiring proprietor will have obtained a valuation for the business being sold.

As a buyer, you should ensure that the valuation has been prepared by a professional valuer and that the state of the business equipment and the income that the business generates have been taken into account.

In the example of JT's Restaurant, Tony has a good knowledge of the market value of restaurant businesses and has managed to obtain what he considers to be a good discount from the current owners.

The purchase price of a business can often be broken down into the following headings:

1. Property
2. Goodwill – this is a premium that is often charged on buying a business (more on this in Chapter 7)
3. Fixtures, fittings and equipment
4. Stocks and consumables

As previously mentioned, JT's Restaurant is being purchased for £120,000, but this amount does not include the property (at this stage), hence the rental cost of £2,000 a month in the forecast.

The £120,000 relates only to the goodwill, fixtures and stocks, and the vendor is negotiable on how that amount is split (this is very relevant for tax purposes).

As a buyer you need to ask yourself the following four questions:

1. Is the value allocated to the property in line with similar local properties, and could a purpose-built property be constructed for less?
2. Has the goodwill been valued by a professional valuer?

The value of goodwill varies from industry to industry and is negotiable. A simple check online can tell you whether the amount being requested is in line with industry averages.

Often, the price being asked for the business goodwill can surprise those new to business, but when that price is compared to the cost of setting up a business from nothing, equipping the premises and attracting a customer base, it often works out quite reasonable.

Somebody else has done the hard work and lived on a low income while the business has built up.

The alternative is for you to do it yourself.

There is a risk in paying for goodwill, as after a sale there is no guarantee that the customers will stay with the new owner, and a provision needs to be made in any purchase documentation to ensure that the vendor doesn't set up nearby and entice his customers back to his new business.

I recommend that the services of a good commercial lawyer are retained when buying a business. They will ensure that a competition clause is included in the agreement, which will prevent the vendor from setting up in a similar trade, within the same geographical area, within a specified time frame.

3. What state are the fixtures, fittings and equipment in? Could you replace with new at a lower cost? Are they subject to any finance contracts?

Banks often offer new business owners financial products at beneficial rates, and it may be possible to obtain a finance deal for new equipment at a low price. This option could be used as a negotiating tactic when finalizing the purchase price.

4. Are the stocks and consumables in a fit state for resale? Do they need a separate valuation? Does the value agree with the business accounting records? How has obsolete stock been accounted for?

In essence, the purchaser needs to check the value of the assets being purchased and ensure that they are in a fit state to be used by the new business. The contract for the purchase of the business will usually include provisions to protect the new owner from any misrepresentation regarding the business assets.

This is another reason to use the services of a good commercial lawyer when buying a business.

Value-Added Tax on a Transfer of a Business

In the UK, businesses are required to register for VAT if they think that their turnover (gross income) is going to exceed £85,000 in the next 12 months.

Businesses that are registered are required to charge VAT on their income and in some cases that can include the proceeds of the sale of the business.

Given that the VAT rate is currently 20% (July 2017), it can have a significant effect on the overall sales price.

The UK government realized that VAT could have a negative effect on the transfer of businesses and introduced special 'transfer of going concern' rules so that no VAT would be charged on sales.

The sales of businesses affected by the rules are typically those where a business is sold as a 'going concern' or where the sale is part of a business that can be operated separately.

The rules basically allow the seller not to charge VAT on the assets being transferred as part of the sale, as long as the purchaser registers for VAT and both parties have agreed that the application of the transfer of going concern rules is appropriate.

It is important to be aware that the transfer of going concern rules are mandatory and not optional. So, it is important to establish from the outset whether the sale is or is not a transfer of a going concern.

The main conditions for a transfer of a going concern are

1. The assets must be sold as part of the transfer of a business as a going concern.
2. The assets are to be used by the purchaser with the intention of carrying on the same kind of business as the seller (but not necessarily identical).
3. Where the seller is a taxable person (i.e., registered for VAT), the purchaser must already be a taxable person or become one as the result of the transfer.
4. Where only part of the business is being sold, it must be capable of operating separately.

The correct VAT treatment on the sale of a business can be significant. For example, the sale of a business for £500,000 plus VAT would need the purchaser to find £600,000 if the rules did not apply.

It is also important to get this aspect of the sale of a business right, as any VAT paid in error cannot be reclaimed.

I strongly advise that specialist advice is sought on this matter, as it can have a significant effect on the amount of finance required to buy the business.

How Should You Finance the Purchase?

Most newcomers to business will not have the funds to buy a business outright and will need to raise funds from an external source to finance the purchase.

It is usual to approach a bank for this funding, but there are now other opportunities available (see the section 'Crowdfunding').

JT's Restaurant is to be funded by straightforward bank borrowing.

Most banks have commercial arms that lend money to businesses, and you will do better approaching them with the mindset that their job is to lend you money (so they need your business!) than approaching them cap in hand.

At one stage, I had a client who had significant bank borrowings. When I asked him 'how do you sleep at night owing the bank all that money?', he replied that he was sure that the bank manager had more sleepless nights because of the excessive amounts he had lent to my client.

I would advise that you take specialist advice when considering financing a business as there are a number of areas that can be confusing.

Advice needs to be taken as to the length of the loan period as there is no point in repaying a business loan (with eligible tax relief) over a short period of time when the borrower also has personal borrowings not receiving tax relief (e.g., a mortgage), which ideally should be paid off first.

In this instance, it is better for the borrower to take the maximum loan repayment period offered and use the extra income that this would free up to pay off the mortgage first.

Following on from the foregoing logic, the borrower should also take the maximum loan being offered.

The borrower should also consider whether an interest-only arrangement should be undertaken in the early years of the loan, as this will reduce the initial cost at a time when cash flow may be tight due to investment in the business.

Taking a loan over a longer period will result in budgeting for lower monthly repayments.

As a result of following the above advice, the borrower would incur interest charges on the borrowing over a significant period of time, but it should be noted that tax relief would most likely be available on those interest charges.

If the business proves successful and finance becomes available at a later stage, the business has the option to repay the borrowings early; however, in some cases, early repayment penalties may be actuated by the restructuring of the finances.

The inclusion of early repayment fees needs to be discussed when initially negotiating the borrowing.

Remember that in addition to the purchase of the business, the purchaser will need to raise an amount to fund the working capital or agree an overdraft facility to finance the business cash flow needs.

In the example of JT's Restaurant, the borrowing required was the £60,000 to buy the business, plus the £20,000 overdraft facility that would be needed to cover the cash shortfall in March in the first year.

Although it is tempting to roll all the finance required into one loan, this is a bad thing for the business to do.

In the preceding example, only £60,000 is needed to be borrowed to buy the business, and if a loan of £80,000 was taken, interest would be payable on the whole amount, including the overdraft element of £20,000 from day one (when the requirement for cash flow funding was actually only short term).

If the overdraft was negotiated separately, interest would only be payable on the amount of the cash shortfall on an actual daily basis.

The difference between the two can be quite significant.

Also, as can be seen from the business plan details in Chapter 12, as part of the deal to buy the business there is a separate deal to buy the property for a fixed price of £200,000 after 5 years of trading, and further borrowing will be required from the bankers to fund the purchase at that stage.

The delayed property transaction is the vendor's decision, and there are advantages to both the purchaser and the vendor in the arrangement.

To the vendor, the advantages are

1. There is no immediate loss in total income as the rental can make up for lost profits.
2. The tax on the sale can be reduced and split over a longer time frame.
3. The vendor has the option to return to the business should the purchaser not succeed.

To the purchaser, the advantages are

1. The financing of the business is easier as the amount being requested is initially smaller, and the second tranche of borrowing may be supported by evidence of profitable trading at that time.
2. It gives the purchaser the option to back out of the property deal if the business does not prove as successful as the vendor is making out.
3. The purchaser knows that the business can afford £2000 a month to finance a loan to purchase the property, as this is what it will be paying in rent (per the cash flow). Given that it is likely that the rental charge will include a premium, it is unlikely that the cost of a loan to purchase the property would cost as much.

(A 10-year repayment loan for £200,000 at 4.5% [1% above the current going rate] would cost the business £2073/month.)

The foregoing detail has been looking at the purchase of a business predominately from a buyer's perspective, but even the new business owner ought to devote some time to thinking about an exit strategy and the best way to sell the business in the future.

If a purchaser agrees to a vendor's requests in an agreement to buy a business, where those requests have been driven by a desire to reduce tax, the purchaser may incur additional taxes upon their own sale in the future.

Often, the structure of a deal to sell a business is governed by taxation, as there are significant differences in the tax that can be payable upon the sale of a business and those amounts can be reduced significantly by careful planning (this topic will be looked at in detail in Chapter 6).

Another thing that needs to be pointed out to purchasers of businesses is that banks tend to look at financing a business as an opportunity to sell inappropriate financial products to the borrower, and the liabilities these can create can affect the future sale of a business.

A decade ago, those businesses which financed themselves at fixed rates, or were persuaded to accept interest rate swaps, did so at significant costs to themselves. But at the time, the sale of the business was something too far away to worry about.

Crowdfunding

The Internet has introduced alternative ways for entrepreneurs and businesses to raise funds for projects if they do not want to use the traditional banking structures.

Given the appalling way that banks treated business owners struggling for finance during the financial crisis in 2008, there has been a strong move away from the financial institutions for business financing.

An alternative to using the banks for funding that is proving increasingly successful is 'crowdfunding', which is a way of raising finance by asking a large number of people each for a small amount of money.

Crowdfunding uses the Internet to put financial propositions to thousands – if not millions – of potential individual funders.

Typically, those seeking funds will set up a profile of their project on a website (in effect a business plan). They can then use social media to raise money.

There are two different types of crowdfunding for businesses: debt and equity.

1. *Debt crowdfunding*: Investors agree to lend the business a certain amount, that amount being specified on the business's online prospectus. After an agreed period of time, the investors will receive their money back with interest. This is also called peer-to-peer (p2p) lending, and it allows for the lending of money while by-passing traditional banks.
2. *Equity crowdfunding*: Under these arrangements, people invest in an opportunity in exchange for equity. Money is exchanged for a share or a small stake in the business, project or venture. As with other types of shares, if it is successful the value goes up. If not, the value goes down.

Various websites, such as www.crowdcube.com and www. kickstarter.com, provide lists of businesses looking for finance, and I recommend that you investigate this topic further if you think you would like to raise finance this way or invest in any businesses currently looking for funding.

I, myself, have investments in a hotel in Valencia and a producer of mobility products for the handicapped in the UK through crowdfunding initiatives. There are endless investment opportunities, and I would recommend, if your business forecasts are robust, that you consider crowdfunding for your own business should your approaches to traditional lenders prove fruitless.

Tax Issues to Consider

If you are going to finance your business by way of a loan, you can include the loan interest in your accounts, which will reduce your profits and ultimately your tax bill.

If you finance your business by providing shares to investors, the payment of dividends to them from the business profits is not allowed as a taxable expense.

What Records Should You Inspect?

You would be foolish to buy a business without checking the financial detail that the vendor has given you.

I would not advise that you examine all the source records of the business in order to audit the income and expenditure levels declared by the vendor, but I would recommend that a clause be included in the sales agreement to the effect that any shortfall in the business income in the years following the purchase could/would result in a proportional refund of the sales price (as long as the shortfall wasn't due to the inaction of the purchaser).

Most businesses use computerized accounting packages which can provide detailed accounts, which are not only useful to the business for management purposes but can also provide a useful source of information to confirm the level of the business income and expenditure upon a sale.

It is usual upon a sale for the latest accounts to be provided by the vendor for inspection.

Following the inspection of the latest business accounts, it is also important to refer to earlier years to ensure that the figures provided are indicative of the usual business performance.

In the case of JT's Restaurant, 3 years accounts of Yoko's Sushi House have been made available for inspection, and nothing is apparent in them to suggest that they are not indicative of the actual trading over those 3 years.

It is also useful to examine the staff contracts of employment to identify whether the current level of pay is in line with that of the last year or so and is in accordance with current legislation.

Identify the long-term employees and be prepared to pay redundancy awards if any of those staff are not needed/compatible following the purchase of the business.

It is usual to lose staff when taking over a business as the new management style may not suit all the employees, so don't be surprised by staff resignations.

All contracts relating to income and expenditure need to be inspected to ensure that they are in the name of the business and will continue to be so following the sale.

Buying a Franchise

An easier but more expensive option for somebody considering setting up a business is to buy a franchise. It is possible to buy the right to run an established branded business, and this is done under a franchise agreement.

With a franchise business, a 'franchisee' licenses the use of trademarks and business methods from a 'franchisor'. Popular franchises include fast-food restaurants. A franchise can be awarded to applicants after a detailed process, which is governed by legislation.

Franchises are a good way to gain business experience with a popular brand because they have existing recognition and proven business techniques.

If you consider that a franchise is the business model you are interested in, a number of steps need to be taken.

1. Find a franchise that fits with your character and your plans. There are agencies that assist franchisees, provide lists of franchises available and advise on the suitability of specific franchises to your circumstances.
2. They can help you decide which one is right for you and can provide details of costs and locations. You will

need to review what financial and human resources you have and how these will fit with the requirements of the franchisor.

To start this process, I would advise that you write to franchisors in the top two or three business sectors that interest you. They will provide you with details of the industry, the company, its business model, the role of the franchisor and the role of the franchisee.

The franchisor will provide all of this in their Franchise Disclosure Document (FDD). This document helps you understand the franchise model, fees and commitments in the franchise agreement.

One of the major benefits of a franchise is that someone else has done the groundwork for you. They have created the concept, researched the market and developed the product, and as part of their agreement they will charge a fee to share their trade secrets, marketing and training programs with you.

The franchisor should provide you with a detailed outline of the kind of support, both operational and marketing, and training you can expect.

You have to pay royalties for using the franchise's trademarks. You should speak to current franchise owners to check that the information the franchisor is providing is correct and to ask what problems they have encountered.

Once you have researched thoroughly, you should ask yourself whether you have the skills and experience necessary to make it succeed.

The franchisor should provide detailed financial information that you must closely study. The franchisor will often have a preferred lender with experience in lending to new franchisees.

How Will the Purchase of a Business Affect Your Tax Bill?

The fixtures, fittings and equipment and stock element of the purchase price of the business will attract a deduction for income tax purposes and assist in reducing the tax liability in the early years in business.

Tax relief on the goodwill element of the purchase price may only be available upon the eventual sale of the business upon retirement.

Likewise, tax relief on the cost of buying any premises may only be available upon the eventual sale at retirement.

Is the Business Right for You or Should You Consider the Alternatives?

Before you commit to buying the business, you need to look at the outlook for the business and the effect any changes in legislation etc. may have upon your future income.

Technological advances may drive your business sector into decline and ultimately bankruptcy.

You need to ask yourself whether the business has the potential to maintain its current level of income and/or has opportunities to grow, in that it has the facilities available and is within an area where a profitable business could be established.

You need to look at the age and health of those you are considering joining with in the business to ascertain whether multiple retirements will be likely in a short space of time, as you may have to find funds to pay those 'partners' out.

You will need to draft and agree a contract with provisions regarding the payout of 'partners' and the obligations of continuing ones.

Is the Split of the Purchase Price Right?

Usually, the price for the purchase of a business will be split between property, goodwill, stock, fixtures, fittings and equipment. The vendor would usually prefer the majority of the sales proceeds to be allocated to the property and goodwill, as the capital taxes on those amounts may be less than the income tax payable on the sale of the stocks, fixtures, fittings and equipment.

But the buyer may normally gain greater allowances to set against his/her income if the sales proceeds are structured the other way round.

The taxation treatment of the sales split may be dealt with differently if a company is utilized to run the business.

As with any business transaction, the valuation provides a figure that can be negotiated up or down, depending upon the willingness of the vendor to sell and the purchaser to buy, and the split of the sales proceeds can often be a negotiating point when reaching agreement on the final sales price.

If the vendor is requesting a split that you consider is unrealistic, remember that you will need to convince the taxman that the amounts are appropriate.

Should You Form a Limited Company to Buy a Business?

There are substantial tax benefits to incorporation for some businesses, but for others the benefits are small and the administrative burden of incorporation too high to make the exercise viable.

The tax benefits can be derived from restructuring the way that business profits are drawn from a company, and the ways of doing this may not suit everyone's needs.

There are differences in the way that incorporated and unincorporated businesses obtain tax relief on the cost of buying a business, and advice should be sought from a specialist in this area.

An example of structuring the purchase of a business utilizing a company is where the ownership of the property and the business are separated (with the option of a rental arrangement being created).

Given this information, it is not possible to give a general answer to the benefits of incorporation, but there are more options to reduce tax by utilizing a company.

Selling the Business

The more profitable sales of businesses tend to be those that are planned, and not as a result of financial pressures. Some sort of plan regarding the sale or succession of the business is, therefore, key to maximizing the eventual sales price, and this is dealt with in Chapter 11.

In order to obtain an acceptable sales price, it may be necessary to put the business on the open market to all comers. To do this, the vendor needs to appoint a specialist agent to market the business and to produce a sales prospectus.

It is key that the vendor is completely open regarding providing details of business performance during the sales process, as any shortcomings will be discovered by the purchasers following the sale and may actuate penalty clauses in the sales agreement.

Also, the vendor is at risk of committing a criminal offense by being less than honest regarding the business's financial position.

Selling an Incorporated Business

There are two ways to sell an incorporated business, and it is important that both the vendor and the purchaser are aware of the differences, as should the wrong option be taken, the tax liabilities can be substantial.

The options are as follows.

1. The sale of the shares in the company, i.e., the sale of the whole company with the business included. In this case, the individual selling the shares receives the sales proceeds.
2. The sale by the company of the business, i.e., the property, goodwill, fixtures and fittings and stock. In this case, the company receives the sales proceeds.

The sale of the shares (i.e., the company) is the preferred option for most vendors, while the purchase of the assets is the preferred route for most purchasers.

The reasons for this are as follows:

1. Tax allowances can be claimed on the purchase of the fixtures and fittings by the purchaser.
2. Tax relief may also be claimed on the purchase of goodwill.
3. Tax relief on the cost of the shares will not be available until their ultimate sale (subject to the reliefs below).
4. The purchaser does not know the history of the company and potential liabilities may arise after the sale that may relate to the period prior to the sale. For this reason, when companies are purchased a detailed investigation is often carried out in order to discover any potential legal claims against the company, etc.

UK Enterprise Investment Schemes

In the UK, the government has introduced the Enterprise Investment Scheme (EIS) and the Seed Enterprise Scheme (SEIS) to encourage investment in small businesses. These schemes provide tax incentives to investors in smaller, unquoted, trading companies.

Enterprise Investment Scheme

The EIS was launched in 1994 and is designed to help smaller, higher-risk companies to raise capital.

It does this by providing the following tax reliefs:

■ Investors can claim income tax relief at 30% on qualifying investments of up to £1 million per annum (which means a reduction of up to £300,000 of their tax liability), subject to the investment being held for a minimum of 3 years.
■ The taxpayer can only claim the allowance if they have sufficient income tax liability.
■ The tax relief applies in the year of investment and/or the previous year.
■ If the investment results in a loss, the loss can be set against the investor's capital gains (more about capital gains in Chapter 6) or his/her income in the year of disposal or the previous tax year.
■ For losses offset against income, should the shares become worthless, the net effect is to limit the cost to 38.5% of the original investment depending on the investor's marginal rate of income tax.
■ Alternatively, the losses can be relieved against capital gains at the prevailing rate of 28%.

These amounts can be seen in the following calculations:

Initial investment	£100,000
Less income tax relief @30%	(£30,000)
Net cost for investment	£70,000

If the value of the investment fell to nil, the net loss to claim against income would be £70,000.

Assuming the taxpayer was paying tax at the additional rate, the loss relief against income at 45% would be	£31,500
Bringing the net loss to	(£38,500)

The percentage of original outlay is 38.5%
Alternatively, if the loss was to be claimed against Capital Gains tax (see Chapter 6 on this tax), the loss could be claimed at the current rate of 28%.

Initial investment	£100,000
Less income tax relief @30%	(£30,000)
Net cost for investment	£70,000

If the value of the investment fell to nil, the net loss to claim against capital gains in this or a previous year would be £70,000.

This could be claimed at the rate of 28%	£19,600
Bringing the net loss to	(£50,400)

Effectively halving the cost of the loss in the investment.

Capital Gains Tax Deferral Relief

Capital Gains Tax Deferral Relief is also available to investors, where it is possible to defer a Capital Gains tax payment on gains arising on disposals of any other assets where those gains are reinvested in new shares in an EIS company.

The chargeable Capital Gains tax is deferred for the life of the investment. The investor can defer gains made in the 36 months prior to their investment or 12 months after.

Inheritance Tax (IHT) Exemption

After 2 years an EIS/SEIS investment qualifies for Business Property Relief (BPR) (see Chapter 6) and therefore can be free from Inheritance Tax (IHT) (again, see Chapter 6).

To qualify for the EIS, the gross value of the company seeking investors must not exceed £16 million (after the investment), and there are restrictions to ensure that the investment is targeted at new risk capital.

The company must also be unquoted on any stock exchange when the shares are issued, have fewer than 250 full-time employees (or the equivalent) and have raised less than £5 million under any of the other venture capital schemes available in the 12 months ending with the date of the relevant investment.

There is no minimum amount that an investor can invest in any one company; however, the maximum investment an investor can make is up to £1 million.

The maximum amount of investment that a qualifying company can receive is limited to £5 million.

Seed Enterprise Scheme

In 2012, the UK government introduced the SEIS, a scheme like the EIS but for startups.

Under the SEIS, a taxpayer may invest up to £100,000 in a qualifying new startup business and be eligible for income tax relief of 50%.

A further relief is given when capital gains are reinvested in an SEIS company (see next section).

The relief is offered regardless of the rate at which the investor pays tax.

The SEIS applies to investment in companies and not unincorporated businesses or limited liability partnerships, and the investment must be in subscription to new shares.

An SEIS company must have less than 25 employees, gross assets of less than £200,000 and have been trading for less than 2 years.

The company should not have already raised funding from venture capital schemes, but it must carry on a genuine new trade and have a permanent establishment in the UK.

SEIS Reinvestment Relief and Capital Gains Tax Relief

To further encourage investors, a Capital Gains Tax Relief is also offered for investments made into new schemes.

Capital gains become tax-free if they are reinvested in SEIS companies to obtain SEIS Reinvestment relief.

The disposal of SEIS shares will be exempt from Capital Gains tax after a 3-year qualifying period.

EIS/SEIS cannot be used to fund the acquisition of a connected existing company or trade. Money received from the investment must be used to promote the growth and development of the business.

This is to prevent investors from utilizing the tax incentives in their own, existing businesses.

Where an investor sells the shares within 3 years for a profit, the tax relief obtained will be withdrawn and an assessment made in respect of the relief given.

In the past, the Tax Authorities held the view that a management buyout couldn't qualify for EIS relief due to the prior involvement of the acquiring managers in the trade, whose ownership is transferred in the buyout. A recent case indicates that there may be ways around this.

As always, expert advice should be obtained on a business purchase or sale and the use of investment tax saving schemes, the rules of which, as can be seen in this chapter, are extremely convoluted.

Chapter 5

Staffing

Your website has gone live and your doors are open, now what do you do? The answer to this is to employ staff to run your business while you spend your time administrating.

The business needs registering with endless bodies, each wanting a cut of your profits for the pleasure. So, you need to get on with the paperwork, or get someone to do it for you.

Before you appoint any staff, you need to be aware that they are key to the business's success, and you need to ensure that they have the personality to fit with your business. They are the face of the business and your customers will associate them with the business.

Staff need to be aware that they only have one chance to make a first impression, and if they are 'front of house' they should know how important they are.

Some businesses assume that anyone can take on the role of receptionist or retail assistant, failing to understand why customer satisfaction is low when no attention is paid to this position.

Staff need to be trained to look at the business from the customer's perspective, and to be educated that their wages are paid (effectively) by happy customers. They need to know that their income is reliant upon the business doing well.

There are a few businesses around where an indolent assistant has made me feel like a nuisance, which I am unlikely ever to visit again. It is probable that the management of those businesses will have little idea as to how they are failing in customer care, as they have not committed any resources to it.

Training is key, and a profit share arrangement is a good motivator in ensuring your business is number one. Encourage an eye for detail, as the little touches make all the difference. Make the staff feel part of a team and include them in a joint vision.

Coaching and mentoring is very important, and you should even be training someone to do your own job, so that at some point you can either:

1. Sit back and watch them earn the money for you.
2. Plan for retirement and succession, so that you have someone tailor-made for a seamless transfer of the business.

But it isn't all plain sailing; dealing with unions and employment legislation is a nightmare, and expert help should be sought to deal with problems in these areas.

Employing staff is an administrative nightmare, and advice is essential in dealing with the payroll procedures.

There are numerous legal hurdles to overcome, such as national living wage, pension schemes, employers' liability insurance and human rights legislation.

Governments are increasingly divesting themselves of the administration of the collections and benefits systems, and this role is becoming the responsibility of employers. The PAYE system is becoming the medium of choice for cost-effectively dealing with those matters.

Setting Wage Levels

Don't be tempted to cut what is most likely your major expense by paying low wages. Remember, 'you pay peanuts, you get monkeys'. If you focus on making your business the best, you should employ the best (most expensive) staff. Don't get greedy, share the spoils... it makes it more fun if you're part of a team.

But don't pay too much, your staff will get lazy if they realize that they don't need to do much to earn a decent living.

So how do you get it just right?

You will need to scan the jobs vacancies advertised (both locally and online) to get an idea of the wage rates you will need to pay. The amounts you will have to pay management, administration and reception staff and retail and production staff may vary.

Given the costs of recruitment, it is important that the right staff are appointed, as the costs and disruption of staff changes can have a detrimental effect on the business. It is important, therefore, to concentrate on the recruitment process. The following mantra will help you avoid the pain of lots of staff changes.

'Interview well, pay well, share the spoils'

Remember everyone has their price.

There are a number of organizations that assist employers in the recruitment process, and it is often worth utilizing their services, especially when recruiting highly paid/senior staff.

If you have decided to incorporate your business, you need to be aware that you may also be an employee if you wish to draw a salary from the company. (There are tax regulations that make this option an administrative nightmare.)

If you are deemed to be an employee of your own company, you are still subject to the same employment legislation as the rest of the staff, and eligible for the same rights.

Staff Pensions

Every business in the UK is legally obliged to provide a workplace pension scheme to make sure that every worker will have the chance to save for their retirement.

This is part of the government's attempt to divest itself of its responsibilities, which include looking after retirees. If retirees have their own pension pots, they can look after themselves (in theory).

Every employer has to give their workers the opportunity to join a workplace pension scheme that meets certain standards.

Depending on their age and income, many workers are automatically enrolled into the scheme, while other workers are entitled to join the scheme if they so wish.

Workers earning over a certain amount are entitled to a minimum contribution into their retirement pot. This can be made up of (1) an amount taken from the workers' pay, (2) an amount paid in by their employer and (3) a further amount from the government, although employers can pay the entire minimum contribution themselves if they want to.

The minimum contribution has been initially set at 2% of the employee's income, with plans to increase it, ultimately, to 8%.

Further details of the workplace pension scheme can be found on the Pension Regulators or the National Employment Savings Trust (NEST) websites.

Please note that the foregoing rules apply to employees only, not self-employed subcontractors.

Self-Employed Subcontractors

Often, a business may need tasks undertaken by individuals who neither the company nor the individual want to become employees of the business.

This may be due to the task being a one-off specialist short-term arrangement, and in these cases the business should check the status and the ability of those involved.

The work may be of such a nature that there may not be employees within the business capable of undertaking the role. If this is the case, the work can, in most cases, be carried out on a self-employed basis.

There are many other reasons why the arrangement would, from the business's viewpoint, be better as a subcontractor one. These are mainly the costs and responsibilities that the business has to shoulder as an employer.

The savings to a business of treating its staff as self-employed are significant, as they do not have to pay maternity pay, sick pay or redundancy payments (in fact, all employee benefits hard fought for and achieved over the last century).

An increasing number of businesses are opting to take advantage of the subcontractor/self-employment rules to reduce their costs and employ staff on zero-hours contracts (where they don't even offer any security of employment at all!).

Examples of the responsibilities and costs that employers can successfully avoid by adopting a subcontractor arrangement are listed next.

The National Minimum Wage

The National Minimum Wage is the minimum pay per hour almost all workers are entitled to by law in the UK.

Category of Worker	Hourly Rate
Aged 25 and above (national living wage rate)	£7.50
Aged 21–24 inclusive	£7.05
Aged 18–20 inclusive	£5.60
Aged under 18 (but above compulsory school leaving age)	£4.05
Apprentices aged under 19	£3.50
Apprentices aged 19 and over, but in the first year of their apprenticeship	£3.50

Employment Legislation

It seems like it's every day that there's a ruling from an Employment Appeals Tribunal, the Court of Appeal, the Supreme Court and the European Court of Justice regarding employment law.

It is very difficult to keep abreast of these changes in employment law, and it is advisable to liaise with your legal advisors on a regular basis regarding updating your procedures.

The larger you get, the more likely you will be to have an in-house team to deal with all employment issues, as to fall foul of the legislation can be expensive.

Employment law covers everything that you are legally obliged to do as an employer, and it also covers the rights of your employees. Keeping up to date will ensure that you protect yourself, your employees, your customers and your business.

Employment law covers every aspect of the relationship between employers and employees, such as

- Employment contracts
- Wages and hours of work
- Holiday and sickness pay
- Discrimination and harassment
- Redundancy, tribunals and disciplinary processes

The laws are often designed to protect employees from unfair practices, but by having watertight employment contracts and procedures in place the business can protect itself.

Employers' Liability

As an employer, you are responsible for the actions of your employees when they are deemed to be carrying out their work for you. If an employee is the cause of an accident or a financial disaster, the employer is held responsible.

Employers' liability insurance protects a business against the cost of compensation claims from third parties and employees for illness or injury sustained as a result of the employee's negligence while working for the business.

It is a legal requirement for all businesses which employ one or more people to have this insurance cover. There are fines of up to £2500 for those businesses that do not insure.

Staff Management

Given the potential costs, a business needs to closely manage its staff to ensure that they are not incurring liabilities by their actions.

An employer needs to put procedures in place to deal with discrimination and harassment and to ensure a culture of bullying does not exist in their workplace.

Staff management can mean dealing with some very basic matters. I, for one, have had to reprimand a male employee on his less than hygienic toilet habits.

The staff management role can also be outsourced to a third party, or in the extreme case, automated. Bridgewater Associates, a leading hedge fund, has recently commenced a project to automate the day-to-day management of the firm, including hiring, firing and strategic decision-making.

Staff Relationships

In a small business, a team works very closely over long hours, and often close relationships can develop. Some of these relationships can become more than platonic and can affect the marriages of those concerned.

It is important that a business recognizes that their working practices can lead to the formation of these relationships and introduce procedures to discourage same.

Though, in my experience, it is often the proprietor and their personal assistant working long hours together, who turn their relationship into one that is not business related.

If anyone within the workplace makes unwanted advances to another there is a danger of employment law being broken. The recent cases of celebrities' inappropriate behavior have highlighted the suffering of the victims.

Statutory Maternity, Paternity, Adoption and Shared Parental Pay

By law in the UK, employers are required to pay the following amounts to their staff (Statutory Maternity Pay has been shortened to SMP):

Type of Payment or Recovery	2017–2018 Rate
Statutory Adoption Pay (SAP) – weekly rate for remaining weeks	£140.98 or 90% of the employee's average weekly earnings, whichever is lower
Statutory Shared Parental Pay (ShPP) weekly rate	£140.98 or 90% of the employee's average weekly earnings, whichever is lower
SMP/SPP/ShPP/SAP – proportion of payments employers can recover from HM Revenue & Customs	92% if your total Class 1 National Insurance (both employee and employer contributions) is above £45,000 for the previous tax year and 103% if your total Class 1 National Insurance for the previous tax year is £45,000 or lower

As you can see from this table, a proportion of the amounts payable can be recovered from the Revenue Authorities through the PAYE system.

However, it still defeats me why the government feels a business should be shouldered with costs because its staff decide to have or adopt a child. Surely it should be up to the parents to decide whether they can afford to raise a child before they consider having one.

Statutory Sick Pay (SSP)

The same weekly SSP rate applies to all employees. However, the amount you must actually pay an employee for each day they're off work due to illness (the daily rate) depends on the number of 'qualifying days' (QDs) they work each week, as follows:

Unrounded Daily Rates	Number of QDs in Week	1 Day to Pay	2 Days to Pay	3 Days to Pay	4 Days to Pay	5 Days to Pay	6 Days to Pay	7 Days to Pay
£12.7642	7	£12.77	£25.53	£38.30	£51.06	£63.83	£76.59	£89.35
£14.8916	6	£14.90	£29.79	£44.68	£59.57	£74.46	£89.35	
£17.8700	5	£17.87	£35.74	£53.61	£71.48	£89.35		
£22.3375	4	£22.34	£44.68	£67.02	£89.35			
£29.7833	3	£29.79	£59.57	£89.35				
£44.6750	2	£44.68	£89.35					

From this sick pay table, it is apparent that the weekly rate has been set at £89.35, irrespective of the number of days normally worked in a week. As I understand it, a part-time worker earning more than £113.00 for one day a week would qualify for sick pay at the daily rate of £89.35, as long as all the conditions were met.

The amount is paid for a maximum period of 28 weeks and is paid once the employee has been ill for four or more days in a row (including non-working days).

You can't get less than the statutory amount. You can get more if your company has a sick pay scheme (or 'occupational scheme') – check your employment contract.

To qualify for SSP you must:

- Be classed as an employee and have done some work for your employer
- Have been ill for at least 4 days in a row (including non-working days)
- Earn at least £113 (before tax) per week
- Tell your employer you're sick before their deadline – or within 7 days if they don't have one

Agency workers and those on zero-hours contracts are entitled to SSP.

Redundancy Pay

Employees are entitled to statutory redundancy pay in the UK if they work for an employer for 2 years or more. The amounts payable are

- Half a week's pay for each full year employed while under the age of 22.
- One week's pay for each full year employed while over the age of 22, but under the age of 41.
- One and a half week's pay for each full year employed when aged 41 or older.
- The length of service is capped at 20 years.
- The weekly pay rate for these purposes has been capped at £489 since 6 April 2017, and the maximum redundancy payout fixed at £14,670.
- Redundancy pay under £30,000 is not treated as taxable income of the recipient.
- Redundancy pay can often be included in the final pay packet, along with the final wages payment and any holiday pay accrued at that date. These final two items are subject to tax and national insurance, however.

Crown servants, members of the armed forces and police services are not covered by the redundancy pay rules.

All the foregoing benefits payable to staff comprise the costs that employers incur in addition to the pension schemes that they are required to provide for their staff.

It is not surprising then that employers adopt a subcontractor arrangement when 'employing' staff.

The savings that employers can achieve by adopting a subcontractor arrangement may be quite significant but 'employee' morale will be low, and there is likely to be an investigation into the business's employment practices by the Tax Authorities.

The distinction between employment and self-employment is not, in all cases, clear cut, and often causes confusion, but it is a matter that the business must get right as the tax and national insurance liabilities of getting it wrong can be significant.

The Tax Authorities make it quite clear that it is the employer's responsibility to correctly determine the employment status of their workers – that is, whether they are employed by the business or engaged on a self-employed basis.

This will depend upon the terms and conditions of the working relationship with the business. We can look at this further in this chapter, where pro forma employment and subcontractor agreements have been reproduced in full.

It is important for the business to get the employment status right as it affects the way tax and national insurance contributions are calculated, and whether or not the business will need to operate a PAYE scheme. A PAYE scheme is used to collect the tax and national insurance deductions taken from the amounts paid to the individuals involved.

If the business does not get it right, not only could they end up having to pay the tax and national insurance that they should have deducted, but interest and penalties on those amounts too.

So, when a business takes on a worker, they are responsible for determining the employment status of that worker: this applies to all workers, whether they are full-time, part-time, temporary or casual.

Employment status is a matter of fact, based on key terms and conditions of the working relationship between the business and the worker, and in most cases those terms and conditions will be reflected in the contract with the worker (an employment contract is a statutory obligation that sets out the relationship between the business and the worker).

So, how does a business determine a worker's employment status? In most cases, the employment status is quite straightforward. As a general rule, a worker is

- *Employed* if they work for the business and don't have the risks associated with running their own business.
- *Self-employed* if they're in business on their own account and are responsible for the success or failure of that business.

The Tax Authorities have also provided further indicators to assist in the decision. An individual is likely to be employed by the business if most of the following statements apply to them.

1. The business can tell them what work to do, as well as how, where and when to do it.
2. They have to do their work themselves.
3. The business can move the worker from task to task.
4. They're contracted to work a set number of hours.
5. They get a regular wage or salary, even if there is no work available.
6. They have benefits such as paid leave or a pension as part of their contract.
7. The business pays them overtime pay or bonus payments.
8. They manage someone else who works for the business.

The use of zero-hours contracts by employers who adopt dubious business practices, and the introduction of the workplace pension may have had an impact upon these indicators, but the overall message remains the same.

If any of the following statements apply, the worker is likely to be self-employed.

1. They can hire someone else to do the work that the business has given them or take on assistants at their own expense.
2. They can decide where to provide their services, as well as when and how to do the work that the business has given them.
3. The business pays them an agreed fixed price – it doesn't depend on how long the job takes to finish.
4. They can make a profit or a loss.

Self-employed individuals are responsible for calculating and paying their own tax and national insurance on any payments they receive.

A worker is still likely to be self-employed if most of the following apply to them.

1. They use their own money to buy business assets, pay for running costs, etc.
2. They're responsible for putting right any unsatisfactory work at their own expense and in their own time.
3. They provide the main tools and equipment needed to do their work.

If it is decided that the worker is an employee, and that worker is the business's first-ever employee, the business will have to register as an employer, so that the Tax Authorities can set up a PAYE scheme for them.

The Gig Economy

The use of self-employed contractors by 'employers' (as discussed above) has become very common, and the term gig economy has been used to describe this phenomenon.

The expression comes from the entertainment sector, where musicians are paid for performing a 'gig' and no further payments/benefits are required once the performance is over.

The self-employment contracts offered by organizations such as Uber are drafted on the basis that tasks being performed by the 'employee' are separate gigs.

As already discussed, this business model introduces a different 'employment' concept compared to that of traditional employment structures. While in traditional industries, workers enjoy the benefits of unionization, healthcare provision and employee rights with regard to minimum wage, contract termination and working hours, employees within the gig economy are perceived as freelancers.

These people do not receive pension benefits or other employee rights and benefits and are often not paid on an hourly basis. Moreover, their payment scheme is linked to the gigs they perform, which could be deliveries, rentals or other services.

Increasingly, this business model, which is convenient for online/hub organizations, is being used. While this is to the benefit of the businesses using the model, it is to the detriment of not only the employee, who is losing employment rights, but also the government, who is losing out on the taxes paid through the PAYE scheme.

Existing employees can be tempted into these subcontractor arrangements, as has happened in the UK healthcare sector, with the employee hourly rate being increased from the savings made in PAYE payments and the reduction of the costs of the employment rights they are foregoing.

The employee sees the short-term increase in take-home pay but fails to notice the withdrawal of their long-term employment rights and pension benefits.

Although this business model is being used by more and more businesses, recent legal rulings appear to be reversing the trend, with full-time freelancers being classified as employees.

Those workers have been awarded regular workers' rights and protections, although recent rulings against Uber in the UK Supreme Court and the European Court of Justice have further ruled against this business model.

But the trend toward a gig economy has begun. A study by Intuit has predicted that by 2020, 40% of American workers will be independent contractors.

There are a number of factors behind this trend, other than the corporate need to increase profits. The digital age has brought with it a workforce that is increasingly mobile, and work can be undertaken from anywhere.

The job and the location have been separated. This means that freelancers can select from temporary projects around the world, and businesses can select the best candidates from a larger pool.

A benefit of the gig economy for the employee is that more opportunities become available as businesses put more jobs out to tender.

Whether you decide to adopt the gig economy business model depends on

- How much you need the money you will save.
- How much regard or little respect you have for your staff.
- Whether you think you could do more with the tax saved than the government would.

Contracts of Employment

A contract of employment is an agreement between an employee and employer which forms the basis of their employment relationship.

A contract of employment does not need to be in writing to be legally valid, it is the actual behavior of both parties which governs its validity.

A contract starts as soon as an offer of employment is accepted. Starting work proves that the terms and conditions offered have been accepted by both parties.

Every contract of employment should include:

- The business's name.
- The employee's name, job title or a description of work and start date.
- If a previous job counts toward a period of continuous employment, the date the period started.
- How much and how often an employee will get paid.
- Hours of work (and if employees will have to work unsociable hours and if that includes public holidays).
- Where an employee will be working and whether they might have to relocate.
- If an employee works in different places, where these will be and what the employer's address is.

As well as the principal statement, a written statement must also contain information about

- How long a temporary job is expected to last.
- The end date of a fixed-term contract.
- Notice periods.
- Collective agreements.
- Pensions.
- Who to go to with a grievance.
- How to complain about how a grievance is handled.
- How to complain about a disciplinary or dismissal decision.

Most employees are legally entitled to a written statement of the main terms and conditions of employment within two calendar months of starting work, to include details of pay, holidays and working hours.

A contract of employment can be varied only with the agreement of both parties.

As the contract will probably be relied upon in the unfortunate event of a dismissal, it is important that it encompasses all possibilities.

In the next section, I have included a pro forma of a contract as provided by ACAS in the UK. This is followed by a copy of a pro forma self-employment contract for comparison purposes.

The pro forma includes the provisions that ACAS feel ought to be included in an employment contract. I would advise, however, if you are considering employing staff that you retain the services of a commercial legal advisor.

PRO FORMA EMPLOYMENT CONTRACT

An outline of a written statement of terms and conditions of employment follows.

1. You (name of employee) .... began employment with (name of employer) .... on (date employment started) ....

2a. Your previous employment with (name of previous employer) .... does not count as part of your period of continuous employment which therefore began on (date period of continuous employment commenced) .... or,

2b. your previous employment does not count as part of your period of continuous employment.
Select a or b as appropriate.

3a. You are employed as a (job title) .... or,

3b. a brief description of the work for which you are employed (brief work description) ....

4a. Your place of work is (address of workplace) ....

4b. you are required/permitted to work at the following places (give details) ....
   * Delete as appropriate.
   And the address of your employer is (address of employer) ....

5. Your pay will be (particulars of scale or rate of remuneration, or of the method of calculating remuneration) ....

6. You will be paid (particulars of intervals at which remuneration is to be paid) ....

7. Your hours of work are (particulars – including details of any normal working hours) ....

8. Your holiday entitlement is (particulars – including entitlement to holiday pay and public holidays. An employer must give enough information to enable entitlements, including accrued holiday pay on termination, to be precisely calculated) ....

9a. In case of incapacity for work (terms and conditions relating to sickness or injury and sick pay) ....
   Or

9b. where particulars of any terms and conditions relating to incapacity for work due to sickness or injury, and sick pay, can be found (refer to provisions of some other document which the employee has reasonable opportunities to read in the course of their employment, or which is made reasonably accessible to them in some other way) ....

10a. Particulars of pensions and pension schemes
....

Or

10b. where particulars of terms and conditions relating to pensions and pension schemes can be found (refer to provisions of some other document which the employee has reasonable opportunities to read in the course of their employment, or which is made reasonably accessible to them in some other way)
....

11a. The amount of notice of termination of your employment you are entitled to receive is (period of notice)
....
The amount of notice you are required to give is (period of notice) ....

Or

11b. particulars of the amount of notice of termination of your employment that you are entitled to receive and are required to give are contained in (refer to relevant legislation, or the provisions of any collective agreement directly affecting the terms and conditions of the employment, which the employee has reasonable opportunities to read in the course of their employment or which is made reasonably accessible to them in some other way)
....

12a. Your employment is permanent – subject to 11 above, to general rights of termination under the law, and to the following (details of any other rights of termination) ....

Or

12b. your employment contract is for a fixed term and expires on (date) ....

Or

12c. your employment is temporary, and is expected to continue for (period of likely duration) ....
This should be used only as an indication of the likely duration.

13. The collective agreements which directly affect the terms and conditions of your employment are (details identifying the relevant agreements, and indicating, where the employer is not a party, the persons by whom they were made) ....

14a. You are not expected to work outside of the UK (for more than one month). Delete words in brackets if they are inappropriate.
Or

14b. you will be required to work in (details of work location outside of the UK) .... for (period of work outside of the UK, where more than one month) ....
The terms relating to your return to the UK are (details) ....
*Select (a) or (b) as appropriate

15a. The disciplinary rules which apply to you are (an explanation of the rules) ....
Or

15b. the disciplinary rules which apply to you can be found in (refer to provisions of some other document which the employee has reasonable opportunities to read in the course of their employment, or which is made reasonably accessible to them in some other way) ....

16. If you are dissatisfied with any disciplinary decision that affects you, you should apply in the first instance to: (name of the person an employee

application should be made to, or position held, e.g., Supervisor) ....

17. You should make your application by (explain how applications should be made) ....

18. If you have a grievance about your employment you should apply in the first instance to (name of the person an employee grievance should be raised with, or position held, e.g., Personnel officer) ....

19. You should make your application by (explain how grievances are to be raised) ....

20a. Subsequent steps in the firm's disciplinary and grievance procedures are (an explanation of the steps) ....

Or

20b. subsequent steps in the firm's disciplinary and grievance procedures are set out in (refer to provisions of some other document which the employee has reasonable opportunities to read in the course of their employment or which is made reasonably accessible to them in some other way) ....

PRO FORMA FREELANCE AGREEMENT

An outline of a written independent contractor agreement follows:

> <Company>
> Independent Contractor Agreement (Contract for Services)
> Arrangements for the Provision of <describe the services to be provided> Services

1. Details of the Parties

> This agreement is made between:
> <enter name and address of the company> ('the Company')
> and
> <enter name and address of the contractor> ('the Contactor')

2. Commencement and Termination

> This Agreement shall be deemed to commence on <insert date> and shall continue until <insert end date> OR <terminated by either party>.
> Either party may terminate this agreement, by giving 10 days written notice to the other party. However, <company> reserve the right to terminate the Agreement with immediate effect if the Contractor breaches the terms and conditions of this Agreement.

3. Services

> <Company> engages the Contractor to provide, and the Contractor agrees to provide, <describe the services to be provided e.g., teaching, caring, fitness etc.> services within the scope of their professional

competence and fully in line with the terms and conditions set out in this Agreement.

The work will be carried out by the named Contractor appointed, who may not sub-contract all or any part of the work to someone else, without the written agreement of the Company.

Details of the services to be provided by the Contractor under this Agreement are outlined in Appendix 1.

4. Terms

The Contractor is an independent contractor and is not an employee of <company>. In this context, the Contractor shall be wholly responsible for all income tax and national insurance and other similar contributions or taxes (together 'Taxes') which may be payable out of, or as a result of the receipt of, any fees or other monies paid or payable by the Company under this Agreement. In the event that the Company is held liable for any such Taxes, then it will be entitled to withhold such amount from any sums remaining to be paid to the Contractor.

Prior to this contract taking effect, the Contractor will provide the Company with appropriate evidence of self-employment status. Normally, relevant correspondence with the Tax Office will be sufficient for this purpose.

The Contractor cannot incur any liabilities or obligations, express or implied, on behalf of the Company unless specifically authorised in writing to do so.

The Contractor shall maintain in force for the duration of this agreement adequate insurance relating to the provision of Services pursuant to this Agreement. Evidence of such insurance cover must be provided to the Company upon commencement of this Agreement and subsequently on request. The Contractor shall indemnify and keep indemnified <company> from and against any and all loss damage or liability (whether civil or criminal) suffered and legal fees and costs incurred by the Company resulting from a breach of this Agreement by the Contractor.

The Contractor shall ensure that any necessary leave for them to enter or remain in the United Kingdom to perform the Services is valid and subsisting and is not subject to any restriction precluding him from performing these Services. Evidence of such rights must be provided to the Company upon request.

In the event that the Contractor cannot perform the Services during any period of this contract for any reason including sickness, the Contractor shall inform the Company by 09.00 am on the first day of non-performance. No fees are payable covering periods of non-performance. The Company reserves the right to terminate this contract should the period of non-performance last more than 5 working days.

The Services in this contract will be delivered by the Contractor over x days/xx hours per week. Normal working times for the Company are <9am to 5pm Monday to Friday>.

The Contractor shall not agree any further work with a competitor to the Company for similar or related work without first receiving the agreement of the Company, and shall not solicit further work from a competitor directly for similar or related work.

Any requests for goods or services that the Contractor receives while working with a client of <company> will be considered the property of the Company, and the information should be provided to them within 24 hours of receiving such a request.

5. Fees

The Company will pay a fee of £xxx per day/per hour for Services under this Contract. The Company is not obliged to provide the Contractor with any other wages, salary, sickness pay, holiday allowance, travel to work costs, pension or any other payments or benefits whatsoever. If the work has been performed satisfactorily in accordance with the terms of this Agreement, payment will be made in arrears within 30 days of receipt of an invoice from the Contractor.

Minor out-of-pocket expenses will be reimbursed on agreement with the Company and on production of appropriate receipts.

6. Confidentiality

In the event of <company> making available confidential information relating to its business, clients or customers in the course of this Agreement, the Contractor will maintain the confidentiality of such information, and will not disclose it to any third parties whatsoever. Furthermore, except in so far as such matters are properly in, or come into the public domain, the Contractor agrees to keep secret and confidential all matters contained in this Agreement.

7. Provision of Workspace, Equipment and Materials

The Contractor will undertake the Services substantially at their own premises and using their own equipment and materials, the costs of which shall be deemed to have been included within the fee indicated herein.

OR

The Contractor will undertake the Services substantially at <a third-party's OR the Company's>

premises and using Company equipment and materials, the costs of which shall be met by the Company. Any space, equipment or materials provided by the Contractor will be minor in scale and nature relative to this Agreement, and no additional costs will be charged to the Company as a result unless agreed in advance.

The Contractor will, upon termination of their engagement, immediately deliver up to the Company all correspondence, documents, and property belonging to the Company which may be in their possession or under their control.

Any materials whether physical, electronic or intellectual created by the Contractor in the course of carrying out Services under this Agreement will belong to the Company which shall retain the exclusive rights to such material unless agreed otherwise in writing by the Company.

APPENDIX 1

Terms of Reference

The Services to be provided by the Contractor under this Agreement are:

This pro forma had been produced by Human Resource Solutions, who provide free human resources services for small- and medium-size businesses.

Chapter 6

Taxes and VAT

The purpose of this chapter is to highlight those areas of taxation that are likely to impact on a business, and to look at the opportunities there are to reduce the amounts that are payable on the income generated by a business.

No one wants to pay tax, but everyone needs to pay their share for society to function. It is only right that those with the most should pay the most.

Luckily, there are numerous opportunities for individuals to mitigate their tax bills, but the problems highlighted recently in Panama show how businesses have abused these opportunities.

Some businesses have reduced their taxes to minuscule amounts, with little regard to the effect it has on their company image and on the ability of society to function.

This abuse has led to the Tax Authorities toughening their stance on tax avoidance.

The taxes payable on business profits are

■ Income tax
■ Corporation tax
■ Value-added tax (VAT)
■ Capital Gains tax (CGT)

And, in theory, you can decide, dependent upon the structure you utilize to run your business, which of these taxes you pay. Obviously, advice from a specialist tax accountant or lawyer will be necessary to enter into a complex tax savings scheme, but often the tax savings made will only just cover the professional fees involved.

Income Tax

Income tax was introduced in the UK initially to provide funding to fight the Napoleonic Wars, and although the rates and types of taxes have changed many times since, the collection of tax is still a popular pastime for the government of the day.

Income tax is raised on individuals; it is a personal tax and is levied as a percentage of the total income after allowances. It is the tax that most business owners pay on their profits, unless they have incorporated. The rate at which tax is levied and the allowances available (currently in the UK – July 2017) are as follows:

Basic rate	20%
Higher rate	40%
Additional rate	45%
Starting rate for savings income	0%
Dividend ordinary rate	7.5%
Dividend upper rate	32.5%
Dividend additional rate	38.1%

A more detailed explanation of the table below, listing tax bands, can be found in the Tax on Dividends section following.

Starting rate limit (savings income)	5,000
Basic rate band	Up to 33,500
Higher rate band	33,500–150,000
Additional rate band	Over 150,000

Income tax and allowances 2017/2018

Personal allowance	11,500
Income limit for personal allowance	100,000
Income limit for married couples allowance	28,000
Marriage allowance	1,150

Married couples allowance for those born before 6 April 1935

Maximum amount	8455
Minimum amount	3260
Blind person's allowance	2320
Dividend allowance	5000
Personal savings allowance for basic rate taxpayers	1000
Personal savings allowance for higher rate taxpayers	500

National insurance contributions thresholds

Weekly lower earnings limit (LEL)	113
Weekly primary threshold	157
Weekly secondary threshold	157

Upper earnings limit (UEL)	866
Upper profits limit (UPL)	45,000 per year
Upper secondary threshold for U21	866
Small profits threshold (SPT)	6,025 per year
Lower profits limit (LPL)	8,164 per year
Employment allowance	3,000 per year (per employer)

Employee's Class 1 contribution rates

Earnings Band	NIC Rate (%)
Below LEL	0
LEL to PT	0
PT to UEL	12
Above UEL	2

Employer's secondary contribution rates

Above secondary threshold (ST)	13.8

Dividends are taxed as the top slice of income. Where the total income is above £150,000, the tax rate on dividends will be at the higher rate of 38.1%.

The personal allowance is restricted for individuals with a net income of over £100,000. For every £2 of net income above £100,000, the allowance is restricted by £1 until it is reduced to nil.

For example, individuals earning over £111,500 will receive half the personal allowance (£5,750).

Individuals earning over £123,000 will receive no personal allowance.

For this purpose, net income means income subject to income tax.

Business proprietors who increase their level of income from £100,000 to £123,000 will effectively suffer a tax charge of 60% on the additional £23,000 of profits.

This is because the £23,000 will attract tax at the rate of 40% as usual, but the loss of personal allowances means that £11,500 of income that had previously been covered by those personal allowances will now also be taxed at the 40% rate. The total tax is £13,800, which is 60% of £23,000, so this band of earnings needs to be avoided.

Given the way that tax is collected, i.e., the collection of the balance due and the payment on account for the next year, the cash cost of these earnings is even higher than 60%, as can be seen next.

1. Tax due on £23,000 extra profits for the year to 31 March 2018 is £13,800 and is payable on 31 January 2019.
2. On that day, the first on-account payment for 2018/2019 will also be due (of half the above balance) of £6,900.
3. On 31 July 2019, a second on-account payment is payable of £6,900. A total cash tax bill of £27,600 will be paid on earnings of £23,000 (120% tax!).
4. The tax on-account payments for next year of £13,800 in total will be offset against the income earned in the next year 2018/2019 (i.e., tax is paid in advance as it is assumed that the same amount will be earned in the next year).

Income tax in the UK is calculated on the income earned in the year ending 5 April each year (the reason why the 5 April date applies is due to the UK changing from the Julian calendar to the Gregorian calendar in 1752! The tax year was adjusted to accommodate the change and has remained the same ever since).

Business owners in the UK need to submit a tax return and calculate the tax due on their income (self-assessment), return their tax details and pay their tax for the year to 5 April each year by 31 January in the following year.

Most businesses will engage the services of an accountant to deal with this task.

Tax on Dividends

If you plan to run your business using a company, it is usual to extract some of the profits by way of dividend payments. In the UK, you do not pay tax on the first £5000 of dividends that you receive in the tax year. This £5,000 is in addition to the personal allowance of £11,500, so a dividend taken from a company of £16,500 would effectively be tax-free, as long as there was no other taxable income received in the year.

This £5000 allowance is due to decrease to £2000 in the future.

Further dividends are taxed as follows: dividends from £16,501 to £33,500 are taxed at 7.5%, from £33,501 to £150,000 at 32.5% and at 38.1% after that.

The company has to pay corporation tax of 20% on the profits of the business, in addition to the above.

Optimum Tax Planning for Directors on Low Earnings

Businesses with lower levels of profits should look at the most efficient way of extracting the profits from their company.

A common strategy used by most business company owners is to take a low salary from the company with the balance of the income they need being made up of dividends. This can work as follows:

1. A small salary is taken, no higher than the personal allowance, so that no income tax is due on the amount.
2. However, the salary needs to be high enough to gain credits for that year for national insurance purposes, i.e., the lower profits limit (above) of £8164, as this will ensure that there is sufficient income in that year to qualify for state

pension and benefit purposes. A small amount of national insurance may be due on the salary (see previous table).

3. The salary is deductible for corporation tax purposes (at 20%), so the company can claim tax relief on the payment while the business owner receives the amount with only minor deductions taken from it.

4. Any extra money that the business owner needs can be taken as dividends, which are not subject to national insurance. These dividends are not an expense of the company, so tax relief cannot be claimed on them.

5. The National Insurance Employment Allowance allows for the non-payment of up to £3000 of employers' national insurance. However, the Employment Allowance is not available where the business owner is the only employee on the payroll, so this allowance is not available to 'one-man band' companies.

6. When the above strategy is coupled with the £5000 tax-free dividends (for both spouses), a significant amount can be taken from the company with only relatively minor deductions.

As always, I would advise that a professional be consulted before embarking on any tax saving exercise.

Any payment made by a company on behalf of its employees or directors is treated as a 'benefit-in-kind' and subject to income tax.

Corporation Tax

Corporation tax is levied on the profits of incorporated businesses, i.e., limited companies.

The rate of corporation tax you pay depends on how much profit your company makes.

In 2015, the UK government announced legislation setting the corporation tax main rate (for all profits except ring-fence profits) at 19% for the years starting 1 April 2017, 2018 and 2019 and at 18% for the year starting 1 April 2020.

In 2016, the government announced a further reduction to the corporation tax main rate (for all profits except ring-fence profits) for the year starting 1 April 2020, setting the rate at 17%.

(Ring-fence profits: There are different corporation tax rates for companies that make profits from oil extraction and oil rights in the UK or the UK continental shelf. These are known as 'ring-fence' companies. They pay corporation tax at the main rate as other companies and also at the rate of 30% on profits in excess of £300,000.)

Corporation tax is self-assessed, similarly to income tax, in that a corporation tax return needs to be completed annually, and the tax calculated by the taxpayer.

The corporation tax return needs to be submitted to the Tax Authorities within 12 months of the year-end date, and the tax calculated thereon needs to be paid within 9 months and 1 day from that date.

There are more complex rules when the business is operated through more than one company, especially when these operate in different countries.

Example of Tax Planning Exercise

While the preceding tables can look confusing, they hold the key to substantial savings. To aid in understanding the following exercise, I have used JT's Restaurant as an example.

The profits of that business are forecast to be accessed by the team as follows:

- Tony the chef to take a fixed salary of £60,000.
- Me to take drawings of £1700/month in the first year, £2000/month in the second year and £2500/month in the third year.

As VAT payments are not allowable deductions for tax purposes, if these are added back then the cash excess each year that will be treated as profit is

Year 1	£33,159
Year 2	£52,999
Year 3	£69,689

These amounts are to be treated as mine, which are in addition to the amounts that I am drawing on a monthly basis.

If we assume that Tony and I are both married, and the income from the restaurant is the only income that Tony and I (and our wives) receive, our tax bills can be calculated as follows:

Year One

1. With myself as a sole trader, Tony on his salary of £60,000 and the wives not involved:

Paul's tax bill	£10,423.60
Tony's tax bill	£13,000.00
Total	£23,423.60

2. The tax bill can be varied if the business is incorporated, and myself, Tony and our wives all take £16,500 in dividends. I will also take a salary of £20,559 and Tony a salary of £27,000 (these amounts have been calculated to ensure that we [and our wives] both receive the same share of income as in the previous first option). The tax bill now becomes:

Paul's tax bill	£2,674.30
Tony's tax bill	£6,400.00
Company tax	£13,200.00
Total	£22,274.30

A tax saving of £1149.30 for the year, which maybe on the face of it doesn't look significant, but, as can be seen next, is an indicator of bigger savings to come.

Year Two

If the same profit withdrawal methods are considered in year two, the taxes are

1. If the business is operated by me as a sole trader and with Tony the chef on a salary:

Paul's tax bill	£19,799.60
Tony's tax bill	£13,000.00
Total	£32,799.60

2. Utilizing a company and paying dividends to spouses:

Paul's tax bill	£10,574.60
Tony's tax bill	£6,400.00
Company tax bill	£13,200.00
Total	£30,174.60

A saving of £2625.00.

Year Three

If we consider the options again in year three, the savings could be

1. Again, if the business were to be run by me as a sole trader with Tony on a £60,000 salary:

Paul's tax bill	£28,875.60
Tony's tax bill	£13,000.00
Total	£41,875.60

2. Utilizing a company and paying dividends to spouses:

Paul's tax bill	£19,650.60
Tony's tax bill	£6,400.00
Company tax bill	£13,200.00
Total	£39,250.60

A further saving of £2625.00.

Overall, the savings for the 3 years could be £6399.30, and this amount would probably increase the larger the profits get.

It's enough for an extravagant holiday (or business conference?) somewhere to celebrate the business's success.

But note that the savings are purely in respect of taxes, and national insurance hasn't been taken into account. The national insurance consequences would need to be examined before the format of the business was altered to gain the tax benefits.

In addition, a number of non-monetary issues need to be addressed when incorporating a business, and the tax savings may be lost if the limited company format isn't considered the best way forward for those involved.

In Chapter 3, I mentioned that there were more hoops to jump through when operating a business through a company, and it is probable that some of the above savings would be needed to pay the higher legal and accountancy fees.

Alternatively, by incorporating a business, the tax savings made could be sufficient to pay the business's annual accountancy fee.

For those of you with an interest in figures, I suggest that you run through the preceding example again and try to calculate the savings figures yourself. The workings for the examples are included in Chapter 12 for you to check your accuracy.

Value-Added Tax

VAT is a tax that is calculated as a percentage of the turnover of a business and is currently (July 2017) charged at a rate of 20%.

VAT was originally a French idea, started in the 1950s. Britain introduced it as part of its condition of joining the European Economic Community (EEC). All countries joining the EEC had to replace their indirect taxes with VAT.

Most countries in the world utilize a VAT method of raising tax; the USA has a sales tax instead. VAT is an important and efficient system, which is why it is used by so many countries.

VAT is levied on a business's turnover after allowing a deduction for the VAT on the expense incurred in creating that turnover, with the business paying over the net amount of VAT.

The business has to calculate the VAT due on a quarterly basis and submit returns summarizing those calculations.

The taxable limits are as follows:

1. You must register for VAT when your VAT taxable turnover is more than £85,000 (the threshold) in a 12-month period.
2. You receive goods in the UK from the EU worth more than £85,000.
3. You expect to go over the threshold in a single 30-day period.

You can get a registration exemption if your turnover exceeds the threshold temporarily, and you can also voluntarily register if your turnover is below the threshold.

You may also have to register if you take over a business that is already registered.

It is relatively straightforward to register, it can be done online in minutes. There are penalties for late registration, so it is vital that you keep your eye on your turnover for VAT purposes.

Current VAT Rates

The standard rate of VAT is currently (July 2017) 20%; a reduced rate of 5% applies to home energy and some other items; and a zero rate applies to food, health and children's clothes.

In order to account for VAT, businesses need to add 20% to the price of their goods and services. From this, they are able to deduct the VAT that they have been charged and return the net figure to the VAT office.

The following is a simplified VAT calculation:

A business buys bicycles for £100 plus VAT and sells them at £200 plus VAT.

VAT on outputs/sales is 20% of £200	£40
VAT on inputs/purchases is 20% of £100	£20
Amount due to HM Revenue & Customs (HMRC)	£20

The quarterly VAT return has to be submitted online, even if the figures mean that there is a repayment of VAT due.

Capital Gains Tax

CGT is a tax on the profit made when you dispose of an asset that has increased in value. Along with Inheritance Tax, it is a tax that is relatively easy to avoid as some disposals are tax-free.

Capital Gains Tax Basic Rules

- A transfer between spouses or civil partners is tax-free (made on a no gain/no loss basis).
- A gift made between connected persons is treated as being made at market value.
- When a disposal attracts another form of tax, such as Inheritance Tax or income tax, credit is generally given so there is no double charge.
- An income tax trading loss may be offset against capital gains.
- Capital gains may be deferred by reinvestment in some cases.
- Non-UK residents are not taxed on gains made on assets situated in the UK (other than residential property), providing that they remain non-resident for a qualifying time period.
- You can reduce your liability to the tax by deducting previous losses you have made on the disposal of some assets.
- Disposal of an asset can be
  - Selling it
  - Giving it away as a gift
  - Transferring it to someone else
  - Swapping it for something else
  - Getting compensation for it, for example, an insurance payout

It is payable on most assets, which include most personal possessions worth £6000 or more (except motor cars). It is also payable on any property you own (that isn't your main home), although it can be payable on your own home if you've let it out, used it for business purposes or it is very large (see Annual Tax on Enveloped Dwellings below).

It is payable on the disposal of shares and business assets, and it is this aspect of the tax that will mostly affect the business owner.

There are a number of significant reliefs that business owners can claim in order to reduce their liability to CGT.

Capital Gains Tax Rates and Bands

In the UK, taxpayers who are liable for CGT get an annual tax-free allowance (known as the Annual Exempt Amount), which is currently £11,300 a year.

Taxpayers only pay CGT if their overall gains in the tax year (after deducting any losses and applying any reliefs) are above this amount.

The rate of CGT payable on a disposal varies, being dependent upon the taxable income of the taxpayer.

Basic rate taxpayers pay 10% of the profits on disposal of all assets (other than residential property and carried interest).

Higher rate taxpayers pay 20% of the profits on disposal of all assets (other than residential property and carried interest).

Carried interest is a financial interest in the long-term gain of a property development.

Gains on residential property and carried interest are taxed at 18% for basic rate taxpayers and 28% for higher rate taxpayers.

But taxpayers don't pay any CGT when they sell (or dispose of) their own home under Private Residence Relief (which is subject to a number of provisions).

CGT of 28% is paid on the profits on the disposal of property subject to the Annual Tax on Enveloped Dwellings (ATED; see details below). The Annual Exempt Amount does not apply to these disposals.

Companies generally pay corporation tax at the rate of 20% on the capital gains they make (including non-resident CGT on the disposal of a UK residential property).

There are separate provisions for dealing with the gains made by trustees dealing with deceased estates.

Capital Gains Tax for People Non-Domiciled in the UK

A non-domiciled individual is a person, currently in the UK, who was born in a country other than the UK, and intends to return to their country of birth.

Non-domiciled individuals do not get the Annual Exempt Amount for CGT purposes if they have claimed the 'remittance basis' of taxation on their income and gains from overseas.

They can claim the 'remittance basis' if they decide that it is beneficial to have their income and gains from abroad, which they bring into the UK, taxed in the UK. If they claim this option, all other foreign income that is not remitted to the UK is not taxed in the UK.

From April 2015, non-domiciled individuals have to pay CGT on gains realized on UK residential property. The gain taxable is restricted to any growth from the April 2015 value. Alternatively, the seller can elect to pay on a time apportionment basis if doing so would be beneficial.

The matter of foreign income and gains is very complicated, and expert advice should be sought at all times.

Annual Tax on Enveloped Dwellings (ATED)

ATED is an annual tax that is payable mainly by companies that own UK residential property valued at more than £500,000.

Property owners need to submit a return and pay the tax due using the ATED online service.

A return is required if the property is a dwelling in the UK, which is owned completely or partly by a

1. Company
2. Partnership where one of the partners is a company

The amount payable is worked out using a banding system based on the value of the property.

Table 6.1   Chargeable Amounts for 1 April 2017 to 31 March 2018

Property Value	Annual Charge
More than £500,000 but not more than £1 million	£3,500
More than £1 million but not more than £2 million	£7,050
More than £2 million but not more than £5 million	£23,550
More than £5 million but not more than £10 million	£54,950
More than £10 million but not more than £20 million	£110,100
More than £20 million	£220,350

Obviously, there is a lot of activity regarding valuations of property on or near these thresholds, i.e., a property valued at £499,950 will pay £31,400 less than a property worth £50 more! and the owners would be keen to keep the value to the lower amount, but to bear in mind the effect this may have on the eventual sales price of the property.

The Tax Authorities can query the value of a property on the return, and charge the tax plus interest and penalties if they consider that there had been a deliberate under declaration of the value.

Stamp Duty Land Tax

Stamp Duty Land Tax is paid on property purchases in the UK. The percentage amount payable depends upon the property being purchased, and whether an individual or limited company is buying the property.

The rates can vary from 0% for lower value residential properties, to 15% (payable by companies).

By way of explanation, the UK housing market, particularly London, overheated in the late 2000s, and many of the previously described provisions were brought in to stop non-UK citizens using limited companies to speculate in the market.

Entrepreneurs' Relief

Entrepreneurs' Relief reduces the amount of CGT on a disposal of business assets to an effective rate of 10% for all taxpayers, subject to a lifetime limit of £10 million. It is available to individuals and some trustees of settlements, but it is not available to companies or some trusts.

In order to gain from this relief, you need to make a claim to the Tax Authorities by the first anniversary of the 31 January following the end of the tax year in which the gain was made. There is a specific form provided for completion and submission. (The HS275 Self-Assessment help sheet is available to download from the HMRC site.)

Husbands, wives and civil partners are separate individuals, and each may make a claim. They are each entitled to Entrepreneurs' Relief up to the maximum amount available for an individual.

Gains that qualify for Entrepreneurs' Relief are taxed at 10%.

The relief applies to assets owned by you personally and used in a business carried on by either (i) a partnership of which you are a member or (ii) your personal trading company or companies.

The above references to 'business' include any trade or profession, but do not include the letting of property (unless this is furnished holiday lettings).

You must have owned the business directly or it must have been owned by a partnership in which you were a member.

Entrepreneurs' Relief is not available on the disposal of assets of a continuing business unless they're included in a disposal of a distinct part of the business, for example, the sale of a half share of a business.

If the business is owned by a company in which you dispose of the shares or securities, then prior to the disposal for a period of 1 year the company must be

- Your personal company
- Either a 'trading company' or the holding company of a 'trading group'

In addition, you must be either an officer or employee of that company (or an officer or employee of one or more members of the trading group)

A company is your personal company if you hold at least 5% of the ordinary share capital and that holding gives you at least 5% of the voting rights in the company.

Once the £10 million lifetime limit has been claimed, business owners can no longer claim the relief on any future businesses they set up.

But the spouse of an Entrepreneurs' Relief claimant can also claim Entrepreneurs' Relief provided they also own at least 5% of the business, and work there in some capacity also.

So, once a business owner has used up their own lifetime Entrepreneurs' Relief limit, they can in theory claim up to a further £10 million by simply transferring their stake in a business to their spouse at least 1 year before they plan to sell the business.

This is an example of how detailed planning for a future business disposal can save significant amounts of money.

Given that this relief is not available to companies, it will have an effect on how the sale of a business is structured if a company is involved.

As always, expert advice should be sought upon a business disposal.

Capital Allowances

Tax relief can be claimed on fixtures, fittings and equipment used in the business, by way of a writing down allowance, and the writing down allowances currently available vary, depending upon the asset type.

The logic behind the allowance is to give tax relief to the loss of value of an asset as it ages.

The rules regarding capital allowances are complex, and advice should be sought before any significant purchases are considered.

National Insurance

In the UK, national insurance is a system of taxes paid by employees and employers, used primarily to fund state benefits.

It was originally a contributory scheme to fund illness and unemployment, but later expanded to fund the state pension and other benefits that have been introduced over time.

Over time, however, the link between the payment of the tax and the purpose it was to be used for has been lost, and the amounts are now lost in general government revenues.

There has been no ring-fencing of the pension element, as you would expect from a contributory pension scheme, and recent reviews of the adequacy of the system to provide state benefits has led to the increase of the state pension age.

National insurance contributions are paid by both the employee and the employer, based on a percentage of the salary paid. The self-employed contribute partly by a fixed weekly or monthly payment, and partly on a percentage of net profits, above a certain threshold (see National Insurance tables earlier in the chapter).

Individuals may also make voluntary contributions, in order to fill a gap in their contributions record and thus protect their entitlement to benefits.

Employee and employer contributions are collected through the PAYE system while the self-employed contributions are collected through the self-assessment system.

National insurance is significant in that it provides 21.5% of the government's revenue.

Inheritance Tax

Inheritance Tax is a tax on the estate, in excess of £325,000, of someone who has died, unless:

1. Everything has been left to the spouse or civil partner of the deceased, a charity or a community amateur sports club.
2. The deceased gives away his/her home to his/her children or grandchildren, when the threshold will increase to £425,000.
3. For taxpayers who are married or in a civil partnership, with an estate worth less than the threshold, any unused threshold can be added to their partner's. This means that the surviving partner's threshold can be as much as £850,000.

Inheritance Tax is charged at 40% of the estate which is in excess of the threshold, for example, an estate worth £500,000 would only pay 40% on (£500,000 less £325,000) £175,000, a total of £70,000.

Inheritance Tax can be reduced to 36% on some assets if more than 10% of the estate is gifted to charity.

In order to stop taxpayers circumventing the rules, any gifts that they make prior to their death, which will reduce the value of their estate, will be added back to be included in the estate value. Interestingly, this excludes gifts to political parties.

There are a number of provisions regarding gifts, and the timing thereof, which make the calculation of estate values a difficult job, only for the professionals.

A number of reliefs are available to reduce the impact of Inheritance Tax, but the one of interest to the entrepreneur is Business Relief, which allows some assets to be passed on free of Inheritance Tax or with a reduced bill.

You can get 100% Business Relief on

1. A business or interest in a business.
2. Shares in an unlisted company.

You can get 50% Business Relief on

1. Shares controlling more than 50% of the voting rights in a listed company.
2. Land, buildings or machinery owned by the deceased and used in a business they were a partner in or controlled.
3. Land, buildings or machinery used in the business and held in a trust that it has a right to benefit from.

The relief is only available if the deceased owned the business or asset for at least 2 years before they died.

Business Relief is not available for assets that

1. Are used in a business that is not operating for profit.
2. Also qualify for Agricultural Relief.
3. Weren't used mainly for the business in the 2 years before they were either passed on as a gift or as part of a will.
4. Aren't needed for future use in the business.

Type	Rate of Relief
A business or an interest in a business	100%
Unquoted securities that on their own or combined with other unquoted shares or securities give control of an unquoted company	100%
Unquoted shares, including shares listed on the Alternative Investment Market (AIM)	100%
Quoted shares that give control of the company	50%
Land or buildings, machinery or plant used wholly or mainly for the purposes of the business carried on by a company or partnership	50%
Land or buildings, machinery or plant available under a life interest and used in a business carried on by the beneficiary	50%

Relevant property must be held for at least 2 years in order to qualify for relief.

Agricultural Relief

- You can pass on some agricultural property free of Inheritance Tax, either during your lifetime or as part of your will.
- Agricultural property that qualifies for Agricultural Relief is land or pasture that is used to grow crops or to rear animals intensively.

Inheritance Tax regulations are complex, and advice should be sought if it is thought that this is a tax you could be subject to.

Chapter 7

Accounts

Every business has to submit an income tax return to the Tax Authorities each year. Therefore, the proprietor will need to prepare accounts in order to identify the taxable profit of the business.

This will often be the prime reason for the preparation of accounts, but there are a number of other reasons why this task is undertaken.

The example of a business plan/finance application in Chapter 12 includes samples of accounts for reference purposes.

Why Do You Need to Prepare Accounts?

Apart from the need to prepare accounts for tax purposes, the other reasons for preparing accounts are as follows.

- The need to prepare a profit and loss account to identify whether a profit or loss is being made, and to establish if the business can afford to pay its overheads.

- The business needs to identify the level of profit being made in order to ascertain an affordable amount for the proprietor to withdraw.
- The production of accounts will allow the proprietor to identify the efficiency of staff and the amounts of profits that can be paid as wages.
- Without the production of accounts and the identification of expenses, it is difficult to ascertain the amounts that will need to be charged to customers to ensure a profit will be made.
- The production of accounts will allow the proprietor to identify whether there are any excess profits that would allow a pay rise to be made to the staff, or additional amounts withdrawn.
- The production of accounts will enable the proprietors to identify the prior shares of income and expenditure that will be due to/from them as part of their partnership or expense-sharing contract.

Often, when a bank loan or overdraft is used to finance the business, the bank may insist on the business submitting annual accounts to them so that they can monitor the business progress against forecasts.

It would be difficult to sell a business without some sort of profit and loss figures to show prospective purchasers, and those with more detailed figures (in a profitable business) will be able to ask more for their business.

What Accounting Records Do You Need to Keep?

While running a business, you will accumulate a lot of paperwork and documentation that you will need to keep so that year-end accounts can be prepared for the business. The more usual records are as follows.

- *Bank statements, checkbooks and paying-in books.* As the analysis and balancing of a bank account are crucial to the preparation of business accounts, it is essential that these records are complete.
- *Petty cash records.* A lot of the day-to-day expenses of a business are paid by way of cash and it is essential that a record is kept of these expenses, whether funded from cash withdrawn from the bank or from cash receipts from customers. It is preferable to bank the receipts from customers intact, as should the Revenue Authorities decide to investigate the business, it will have a clear audit trail of the receipts from customers being banked. The downside to this approach is that it is quite expensive for a business to bank cash, so it is cheaper to use the cash received to fund cash expenses.

   It is expensive for a business to bank cash as the banks charge fees for this service.
- *PAYE/wages records.* The amounts paid to staff represent the net wages they receive after deduction of PAYE and pension contributions etc. In order to ensure that the accounts are complete, those net wages need to be grossed up from the PAYE records etc., so that the gross cost is included.

   As wages are usually paid one month in arrears, for completeness the post-year-end details need to be included in the accounting records.
- *Purchase and expense invoices.* Invoices for all purchases need to be retained by the business and submitted to the business's accountant, along with the accounting records. The reason is that different tax allowances are available for different types of expenditure, and the details of the type of expenditure are usually found on the invoice.
- *Details of income and expenses allocated to specific proprietors.* In expense-sharing arrangements, certain elements of income and expenditure are identified as

belonging to individual proprietors, and are shown as such in the business accounts.

- *Stock records.* To ensure that the business has sufficient stock and can identify the unsold stock for the year-end accounts, some type of stock record needs to be kept. For smaller businesses, the system can be quite basic, while larger businesses would normally have computerized records to keep track of stock.
- *Expenses paid personally.* Often, when away from the business, business proprietors will buy items for use in the business and will pay the amount due from their own resources. These items need recording or tax relief will not be given on the amounts.
- *Personal use of business expenses.* There are a number of areas of expenditure where there is an element of both business and personal use (e.g., motor expenses), and it is important to identify the personal element that needs to be excluded from the accounts.
- *Statements from suppliers.* It is especially important to keep these at the year-end date so that the creditors (the amounts that the business owes) can be identified for the accounts.
- *Details of income owed to the business.* To ensure that customers pay, it is important that the business has some way of identifying the unpaid income of the business at any given time. This is especially important at the year-end date as these amounts need to be included in the accounts.

This list represents the basic source documents from which the business accountant will prepare the business accounts. While there are a few businesses that will deliver those records to their accountant and ask them to prepare their accounts from those source documents, most businesses will have completed some bookkeeping procedures prior to submission in order to reduce the work the accountant has to do.

The main reason for this would be to reduce the accountancy costs, which could be significant given that the accountant will charge an hourly rate for the work done.

The source documents need to be kept for at least 6 years, and be available for inspection by the Tax Authorities at all times.

Bookkeeping and Management Accounts

By completing some bookkeeping procedures, the business will (i) reduce the accountants' charges for the production of the year-end accounts, (ii) ensure that correct payments are made to staff and suppliers and (iii) ensure that all amounts due to the business are received.

The minimum bookkeeping procedures to put in place or to expect from an agency providing bookkeeping services are

- To regularly balance the analysis of the bank transactions with the bank statements, usually monthly.
- To provide a list of suppliers that need paying at the end of the month, and write checks or prepare bank automated clearing services (BACS) or similar banking instruction for automatic payment.
- To provide a list of outstanding amounts due to the business each month, in order that the business staff can take action to collect those amounts.

The analyzed and balanced bank account summary will be the key document provided to the accountant at the end of the year for the purposes of preparing the accounts.

Some bookkeepers will also provide a payroll service to assist businesses with the paperwork necessary to process the payment of wages to staff. The rate of pay for a suitably qualified bookkeeper is in the region of £15/hour, or an online bookkeeping service for £30/month (in the UK).

Given the foregoing cost, a number of businesses will use a member of staff to complete the bookkeeping procedures, or in most cases the proprietors will complete the procedures themselves. If a business uses a member of staff to keep its books up to date, it needs to bear in mind the following:

■ Would the member of staff be more efficient in their original intended role, and would the cost of a bookkeeper be more or less than the cost of taking that member of staff away from their other duties?
■ Has the member of staff got the ability to do the task at the same speed, and as efficiently as a bookkeeper?
■ Would the use of a member of staff present problems with confidentiality as to the proprietor's level of earnings and withdrawals from the business?

Bookkeeping can be undertaken manually in a cash book (increasingly rare), on an Excel spreadsheet or on a computerized accounting package, such as Sage or Quickbooks.

A number of businesses which employ a bookkeeper, or who have more advanced accounting skills, prepare management accounts regularly (either monthly or quarterly) by utilizing one of the aforementioned computer packages. Management accounts can show the business its level of profitability and solvency throughout the year by effectively producing an income and expenditure account and balance sheet at given dates.

It is not necessary for a business to prepare management accounts unless:

■ The level of bank funding is high, and the bank requires regular management accounts as a covenant of the loan agreement.

- The business is new, or has cash flow issues which require it to keep a firm grip on the finances.
- The business is large and/or has a profit/expense-share calculation which is dependent upon regular updates of the level of income and expenditure.

One task that should be subcontracted to a bookkeeper or accountant is that of the completion of the payroll records, as these are becoming increasingly difficult to keep. The reason for this is the move to process the payment of benefits and the collection of debts through the PAYE system. The weekly or monthly pay run can be complicated by the payment of working tax credits and maternity and paternity pay, and the deduction of student loans and other debts.

What Do the Accounts Look Like?

Usually, the first schedule in a set of accounts is a detailed summary of the income and expenditure, which is often called a profit and loss account, as this schedule summarizes the profit or loss made by the business in the selected period.

The following table (Table 7.1) shows a typical business profit and loss account. The figures included in the account are not intended to represent any industry averages, but provide ballpark figures purely for the sake of the example.

Profit and loss account example

Income

As you can see from the account, the income of the business is usually shown at the top of the schedule and will typically be made up of amounts received (and receivable) from the business sales.

Table 7.1   Profit and loss account example

	£	£
Income		414,000
Expenses		
Cost of sales	161,000	
Wages and salaries	64,000	
Recruitment costs	800	
Courses and staff training	500	
Rates and water	3,000	
Light, heat and power	3,500	
Use of home as office	1,000	
Repairs and maintenance	7,000	
Telephone	3,000	
Printing, postage and stationery	5,000	
Subscriptions	2,000	
Equipment leasing	15,000	
Sundry expenses	5,000	
Insurance	3,500	
Motor expenses	500	
Advertising	6,000	
Accountancy	3,000	
Legal and professional fees	500	
Bank charges	500	

(Continued)

Table 7.1 (Continued)   Profit and loss account example

	£	£
Credit card charges	2,500	
Depreciation charges	5,000	
Bank loan interest	14,000	
Hire purchase interest	3,000	
		309,300
Profit for the year		104,700

Expenses

A business will incur many different types of expenditure. The more usual expenditures are as follows:

- *Cost of sales*: This category of expense usually relates to the cost of the items that have been sold. In addition, this category includes all the consumables used in the sales process, such as dispatch costs.
- *Wages and salaries*: This category is usually a significant cost in most businesses. This expense represents the gross salaries agreed payable plus employers' insurance costs, pensions and any other costs of employing staff.

  If the business has incorporated (i.e., operates as a limited company), the wages and salaries expense will often also include the proprietors' salaries (and spouses if appropriate).
- *Recruitment costs*: The costs of recruitment can be quite high, especially when advertising higher paid posts in the trade press. Even advertisements in the local press for administration staff vacancies can prove costly. If these amounts are not distinguished from general advertising costs, the benchmarking process can be adversely affected.

Occasionally, the business may use an agency to source staff members, and the fee payable for this service would also be included within recruitment costs.

■ *Courses and staff training*: Most businesses will benefit from their staff undertaking continuing professional development (CPD), which may cover areas such as basic customer care or the latest technological advances. The costs of this training may, in some cases, be quite significant.

■ *Rates and water*: Most businesses will be assessed for business rates, and that assessment will take into account location, property values and local economic conditions, among other factors dictated by government policy. The amount assessed will be payable to the local council.

In addition, the business will also pay water rates to a utility company.

■ *Light, heat and power*: This category of expense will include the costs of gas, oil and electricity. This is often a significant expense for a business.

■ *Use of home as office*: Often, the proprietor of a business will do a significant amount of work from home, whether it is dealing with suppliers or dealing with administration and financial matters. In addition, many business proprietors keep themselves updated by undertaking research on the Internet. As a result of these activities, they often incur additional expenses in their home, and it is these expenses that can be claimed as an expense against the business income.

■ *Repairs and maintenance*: Many items owned by a business need maintaining, thus service or maintenance agreements are taken out with manufacturers and suppliers of that equipment.

The expense of these agreements plus the cost of general repairs within the business are included within this category. However, any items of material value that are replaced would usually be shown within the equipment heading on the balance sheet (see later notes in this chapter on the balance sheet).

■ *Telephone*: This category of expense would usually include the costs of the business landline and broadband, plus on occasions a proportion of the proprietor's home, mobile phone and broadband costs incurred on business matters.

■ *Printing, postage and stationery*: The cost of printer toners can account for a significant amount of this expense. This category also includes the costs of producing business-headed paper and associated stationery, postage of letters, etc.

■ *Subscriptions*: To keep up to date with business sector advances, most businesses join trade associations and other such bodies. The subscription costs, either upon joining or the annual subscription, can be quite significant.

■ *Equipment leasing*: It may be financially advantageous to lease the business equipment rather than buy it, as lease payments are allowed as an expense against the business income. Under a lease, the ownership of the equipment remains with the leasing company, and the business pays a rental while it effectively hires the assets.

■ *Sundry expenses*: The expenses within this category are usually smaller amounts that do not fit within another category. Examples of usual expenses posted to sundries are refreshments, newspapers and magazines, window cleaning, staff parties and entertainment.

■ *Insurance*: This expense heading will include the insurance costs for the following:
    – Buildings
    – Contents
    – Public liability
    – Professional liability (if appropriate)
    – Employers liability

– Motor insurance (may alternatively be included in
motor expenses)

Often, a proprietor may take out insurances to protect
his income in the event of illness, or a life policy to repay
loans etc. upon death. Depending on who the beneficiary of these policies is, the expense may not be allowed
as a business expense, but charged to the proprietor as
a personal expense.

■ *Motor expenses*: The costs of running the business's vehicles, and the business element of the proprietor's vehicle.
The home-to-work trip for the proprietor or any staff with
company cars is not allowed as a business expense, so
only the motoring costs for visiting customers and suppliers, exhibitions, conferences and courses, and visiting the
bank and professional advisors are allowable.

■ *Advertising*: Most businesses will have to incur advertising costs to attract new customers, whether this is in the
traditional press or click-linked based advertising online.

The business should ask every new customer how they
found out about the business, as this information is crucial to assess the effectiveness of the business's advertising strategy. Many businesses do not do this and waste
large amounts of money on ineffective advertising.

In the accountancy profession, for example, research
has shown that in some cases fewer than 1% of new
clients join the practice as a result of an advert in Yellow
Pages, but many firms are unaware of this and spend
thousands each year on expensive adverts in telephone
directories.

■ *Accountancy*: The cost of preparing the business
accounts and the proprietor's tax returns is often shown
as an expense of the business, but there are some
businesses that treat the individual proprietor's tax
costs as their own, and do not include them within the
accounts.

The accountancy costs should remain fairly static, except when advice is needed on changes of proprietors, property issues and tax-planning arrangements.

■ *Legal and professional fees*: From time to time, the services of professionals may be needed, whether it is a solicitor drafting a new partnership agreement or a surveyor providing a valuation of the business premises. These expenses will often be shown in the profit and loss account, but sometimes they may not be allowed as a tax-deductible expense given that they may relate to a capital project, such as the purchase of a property.

■ *Bank charges*: Most banks will provide free banking to new businesses for a period, but thereafter will calculate charges based on the number of items being paid in and out of the business bank account. It is worth exploring the options available, and free banking for the longer term should be available to businesses who do not need to borrow any money.

■ *Credit card charges*: Most customers tend to pay for their purchases by way of credit card, and it is essential that businesses provide the facilities for this type of payment. Only a small number of financial institutions provide these services and the costs they charge are very similar, and substantial.

Businesses are charged a percentage of their sales income, with the percentage charged based on the annual sales income. Basically, those businesses with a higher amount of credit card sales will pay a smaller percentage fee.

■ *Depreciation*: This is a non-cash expense often added to the accounts by the accountant while preparing the year-end accounts. The purpose of the charge is to show the decrease in the value of assets over time, and is usually charged as a fixed percentage of the cost of the asset each year. The rate of depreciation charged will depend upon what type of assets the business owns. For example, computers are often charged with 33.3% depreciation in order to write them off over 3 years.

■ *Bank loan interest*: The interest on any business loans can be included in the profit and loss account as an expense; however, the capital element of the repayment cannot.

■ *Hire purchase interest*: A hire purchase agreement is effectively a loan agreement, usually with a finance company allied to one of the main banks. Often, the rates charged can be in excess of those offered by the banks, except when the manufacturer of the equipment being purchased subsidizes the arrangement with a low rate of interest.

The names applied to different financial arrangements are many, but the basic concept remains the same, and the interest or hire charge element of the repayments is allowed as expenses against income.

The profit for the business is calculated by deducting all the aforementioned expenses incurred from the business income. The amount of profit varies significantly between different business sectors.

What Level of Profit Will You Make?

The answer to this question is basically up to you. How hard do you want to work? What motivates you? The level of profits you make will be dictated by the demand there is for your business, and how much money you want to make.

What Should You Do to Protect Your Income?

Those new to business should look at the liabilities (both business and personal) that need to be paid regularly and assess how long they could survive on a reduced (or nil) income as a result of an illness. This is an essential exercise as any financial problems of the proprietor soon have an impact on the business.

A principal will, therefore, need to make the following provisions:

1. *Locum cover.* A policy which provides funding for someone to undertake the principal's role within the business, should he be incapacitated. This will ensure that the business continues to trade in the event that the principal is ill.
2. *Business expenses policy.* Should a locum not be found or if the business is considered that personal to the principal, an alternative arrangement would be to provide for the business overheads to be paid. This type of policy would normally pay out a fixed amount based on the level of expenses in the latest set of business accounts.
3. *Critical illness policy.* This policy can provide a personal income in addition to the above and would usually provide for the proprietor to receive a fixed level of monthly income for life (or until the receipt of pension). The amount of income will usually be based on the after-tax level of drawings of the principal.
4. *Life cover.* This policy will pay out an amount to repay the bank borrowings upon death should the business consider the short-term repayment of capital to the principal's executors a problem.

Tax Enquiries

The foregoing profit and loss information is useful for business owners to benchmark their performance against industry averages (if these have been prepared by industry specialists), and also provides the basis of the information that will be returned to the Tax Authorities. This is done by completing a tax return.

Once the return is completed, it will be submitted, probably online. Upon submission, the return is not usually checked by the Tax Authorities, but may be selected by exception reporting if it appears that items are omitted, or figures do not conform to those expected from a business in that sector. If a return is selected at this time, it will be subject to an aspect inquiry, which will usually be closed if a satisfactory answer to the query can be provided.

If a satisfactory answer cannot be provided at this stage, it is likely that a full inquiry will be initiated into the tax return, which may involve all the business records being requested.

If, following the investigation, the Tax Authorities find personal items being claimed for in a cavalier fashion or find significant under declaration of income, they have the right to investigate other years, and assess for the amount of tax they consider underpaid, along with interest and penalties.

Along with the costs of the tax and penalties, a tax investigation will generate a significant cost in terms of professional fees, so it is best avoided. There are a number of ways to reduce your tax burden legally, and these are looked at in Chapter 6.

The foregoing accounts concentrated on the income and expenditure of the business, but there is another element to a business's accounts called a balance sheet, which focuses more on what the business is worth.

The Balance Sheet

In order to get a complete picture of your financial position, you will need to have a balance sheet prepared. A balance sheet is made up of the following two parts.

1. A list of assets and liabilities that comprises the total worth of the business.
2. A capital/reserves/current account that equates to the list of assets and liabilities (hence the expression 'balance sheet').

An example of a balance sheet is shown in the following section, and the following notes provide explanations of the figures and the descriptions more commonly used by accountants.

Fixed Assets

Fixed assets comprise assets such as goodwill, property, plant, fixtures and equipment. The term 'fixed assets' is used in accountancy to describe assets and property that cannot easily be turned into cash.

These can be compared to current assets, such as stock, debtors, cash or bank accounts, which are described as liquid assets as they represent cash or items that can quickly be converted into cash.

The fixed assets that are usually found on a business balance sheet are goodwill, property, fixtures and equipment, and in some cases motor vehicles. Further details of these assets can be found in the following sections.

Fixed assets can be further divided into two subclasses: tangible and intangible assets. The tangible assets are those you can touch, such as property and equipment and so on, and intangible assets usually comprise goodwill and intellectual property. The intangible asset on the following balance sheet (Table 7.2) represents the goodwill of the business.

Goodwill

Upon a sale or transfer of a business, it is common for the proceeds to exceed the value of the tangible assets of the business. This excess payment or premium represents the 'goodwill' that will need to be paid to the proprietor selling the business, in order to buy the rights to the future profits of the business.

Goodwill is calculated by reference to the continuing business that the organization is likely to retain after the sale or transfer. The level of goodwill is dependent upon the level of business profits, with the more profitable businesses achieving higher levels of goodwill upon a sale or transfer.

The goodwill in the previous balance sheet example is £250,000.

Table 7.2   Example of a business balance sheet

	2017		2016	
	£	£	£	£
Fixed assets				
Intangible assets		250,000		250,000
Tangible assets		450,000		450,000
		700,000		700,000
Current assets				
Stocks	3,500		3,200	
Debtors	17,500		18,300	
Cash at bank and in hand	34,500		43,500	
	55,500		65,000	
Current liabilities	22,500		46,500	
Net current assets		33,000		18,500
Long-term liabilities		235,000		250,000
Net assets		498,000		468,500
Financed by capital and current accounts		498,000		468,500

Goodwill Valuations

The value of the goodwill of a business will not only depend upon the level of profits, but also the following:

1. The level of turnover/total sales.
2. The variety of different sources of sales.
3. The opportunities the business has to expand.
4. The ability of the staff employed.

5. The age and condition of the business's fixtures and equipment.
6. The type of property from which the business operates.

From these factors a valuation can usually be made, but whether that amount is obtained upon a sale will depend upon the eagerness of the vendor to sell and the purchaser to buy. As always, a sale will be subject to market forces.

To maximize the goodwill you obtain on a sale or ensure that you pay the right amount upon a purchase, it is imperative that you secure the services of a specialist valuer. You can often find details of these in the trade press.

If you attempt to save money on professional fees by employing a non-specialist business valuer, you may pay dearly in the long term. Specialist valuers will hold benchmarks of goodwill valuations, which will not be available to the non-specialist.

Accurate valuations are not only necessary upon a purchase or sale, but upon the transfer of the business upon incorporation (where the Tax Authorities may take an interest in the values), or as part of a legal dispute, and when the business is breaking up.

As mentioned previously, goodwill is an area where the Tax Authorities take a keen interest, and it is paramount that specialist advice is sought regarding the valuation of goodwill.

Property

The property that will usually be found on a business's balance sheet will be the premises used by the business and will more often be shown at cost price.

The purchase of a business will often include the purchase or the assignment of a property, which will usually account for a large part of the purchase price.

In order to avoid the more common property pitfalls, it is essential to obtain specialist legal and taxation advice prior to the purchase.

A specialist adviser will have experience of all the things that can go wrong with property ownership and can advise accordingly, whether it is to reduce the tax upon the eventual sale of the property or to preserve the rights of all parties to the agreement.

What Type of Property Is Best for Your Business?

The type and standard of accommodation used by businesses can come in many forms. The more usual are as follows:

1. Converted residential or commercial property
2. Premises in purpose-built retail shopping areas
3. Purpose-built commercial property on industrial estates
4. Use of own domestic premises

The more common premises for business startups tend to be converted houses, shop units or small units on industrial estates.

Whether viewing a business to purchase or another property to move into, the following issues need to be taken into account:

1. The area in which the property stands can affect the type of business that can be run from it, with more deprived areas offering fewer opportunities for more expensive products. These areas tend to bring with them a higher cost in securing a property, with bars on windows and heavy-duty locks needed to protect the property from break-ins.
2. The accommodation that the property provides can affect the business's ability to generate a decent level of profit.
3. A restriction on the available space can limit the business's ability to expand and increase its income.
4. Do legislative changes (such as disabled access, etc.) preclude the property being used for its intended purpose?
5. Older properties and listed buildings can be a headache if planning permission is needed to obtain clearance to use the property.

6. If work is needed to bring the property up to the standard required, this needs to be factored into the offer made for the property.
7. Purpose-built properties tend to provide the best facilities but come at a cost.
8. Some properties are easy to sell: when buying it is advisable to think ahead and try to identify if there are any negative aspects to the property that may affect its eventual sale. (Consider neighboring properties and the area it is situated in.)
9. Will the property be suitable for the type of customer you are trying to attract?
10. Does the property provide good access for customers, in terms of disabled access and parking facilities?

Remember it is better to buy the worst house on the best street than the best house on the worst street.

Freehold or Leasehold: Should You Buy or Rent?

The distinction between freehold and leasehold property can be explained by the following definitions.

Freehold any interest in real property which is of uncertain or undetermined duration (having no stated end), as distinguished from a leasehold which may have declining value toward the end of a long-term lease.

Leasehold an estate, or interest, in real property held under a rental agreement by which an owner gives another the right to occupy or use land for a period of time.

Leasehold property can be further defined as

■ Short leasehold where the portion of the term remaining unexpired under the rental agreement is less than 5–10 years.
■ Long leasehold where the portion of the term remaining unexpired under the rental agreement is more than 10 years.

This distinction between short and long leasehold is not cast in stone, as different industries have their own classifications; for example, residential lets over 12 months can often be classed as long term!

It would be usual to pay a premium to buy a long leasehold as it effectively gives one the right to occupy a property for a substantial period; for example, there are long leasehold properties with leases of 999 years (effectively a freehold). Long leaseholds of such length are generally treated in the same way as freehold properties.

Famously, Arthur Guinness signed a lease for his brewery in Dublin in December 1759, for an annual rent of £45 a year for 9000 years. In retrospect, his landlord appears to have been badly advised at the time.

The company has since bought out the originally leased property, and during the 19th and early 20th centuries the brewery owned most of the buildings in the surrounding area, including many streets housing brewery employees and offices associated with the brewery.

It would be unusual to pay a premium for a short leasehold as it does not provide safety of tenure past the date of termination of the short-term rental agreement.

The exception to this rule is where a fee is paid for a short-term pitch at a sporting/music event for the purpose of providing refreshments. In these circumstances, the levels of profits over the short period are relatively high, hence the premium being charged.

The following issues need to be taken into account when deciding whether to buy a freehold or rent a leasehold property.

1. *Risk*: There is a school of thought that it is riskier to sign a mortgage deed and purchase a freehold (as the mortgage could be a 'millstone around your neck') than it is to sign a leasehold agreement.
2. My personal view is that it is a lot riskier to sign a long leasehold, say for 25 years, as the landlord can claim rent

from you for the whole of the period of the lease, even if you have retired before the end of that period and assigned the lease to your successors! At least if you have purchased the property, you will have the option to sell it to pay off the mortgage.

3. *Freehold property ownership problems*: Where more than one person owns a freehold property, the owners will hold it as either:

   Tenants in common: Each of the property owners own an agreed share of the property. That share can be bequeathed to dependents in a will.

   Joint tenants: The property owners own all the property together. If one of the owners passes away, the surviving owners automatically own all of it, no matter what it says in the deceased's will.

   It is therefore important for the proprietor's family that a commercial property is held by the principals as tenants in common.

4. *Advantages*: Taking on a lease rather than buying a freehold property can be of benefit in the following circumstances:
   - Where there are no suitable properties in the chosen area.
   - Where there are no funds to pay a deposit on the purchase of a property.
   - Where there are no long-term plans to stay in that location.
   - Where the retiring principal is not willing to sell the freehold to the purchaser.

5. *Disadvantages*: Leaseholders, however, suffer the following disadvantages.
   - The payment of rent, although allowable as a taxable expense, is effectively dead money.
   - The repayments on a loan to purchase a property will often be of a similar amount as the rental that property would attract. It is therefore often better to purchase a property with a loan, as the repayments will

help buy an investment that should increase in value over time.

- The leaseholder will ultimately not benefit from the increase in value from any improvements that he or she makes to the property. This is often a reason why leaseholders do not make significant improvements to rented property.
- The leaseholder may be prohibited from extending or developing the property, which may impact upon the growth of the business.
- There may be aspects of the expenditure that the leaseholder incurs on the property that may not be allowed as a taxable expense, whereas if the property was owned these expenses would be allowed against any future capital gain made on the sale of the property.
- The leaseholder will ultimately have to vacate the premises at the end of the lease period, unless the lease provides otherwise.
- Accounts anomalies may arise in writing off the costs of improvements to the property, as there will be no net worth to the leaseholder.

Sale and Leaseback of Property and Gearing

There are financial institutions that specialize in buying profitable commercial premises and renting them back to the businesses that operate from them. These schemes offer taxation benefits to the parties involved and are often restricted to larger more valuable properties.

The advantage to the business owner of this type of arrangement is that the capital investment in the property is released and paid back to them to be available for other business or non-business use. The advantage to the property investor is a long-term investment in a property with the receipt of a rent in the interim.

The disadvantage to this sale and leaseback arrangement for the business owner is that they have lost any share in the growth in value of the property, and they will also lose out on any increase in value that would arise from any improvements they make to the property.

The business owner can also use their property another way, by reviewing the amount of equity they have tied up in the property, and increasing the level of business mortgage they have, in order to withdraw that amount. This procedure is known as 'gearing'.

The higher the amount of equity the business owners have in the property, the more interested the financial institution will be in lending

An example of gearing is summarized next.

A business owner owns premises valued at £1,000,000, with a commercial mortgage of £600,000. His bankers inform him that they are willing to lend up to 80% on property loans.

He increases his business loan to £800,000 and uses the £200,000 released to buy three buy-to-let residential properties, which were priced at £450,000. He borrowed a further £250,000 in order to do this.

Before the financing, he owned properties of £1,000,000, which were mortgaged to £600,000, i.e., he had net equity of £400,000. After the deal, he owned properties worth £1,450,000, with mortgages of £1,050,000, and his equity remained the same.

As long as the tenants provide sufficient income to pay the additional borrowing of £250,000, he has potentially increased his worth by £450,000 by utilizing the £200,000 tied up in the business.

Many property tycoons have used this principle to amass fortunes.

Given the above, a refinancing of the equity is the more preferable option to sale and leaseback should the business wish to release capital tied up in the business.

Who Should Own the Property?

Although it would be sensible for the business owners to own the business premises, there may be tax advantages where limited companies or pension funds (under the control of the business owners) take ownership.

In these cases, the business may be able to claim tax relief on the rentals paid, and the rentals received could be taxed at lower rates than those paid by the business owners, or be received tax-free.

I sold my share of my business premises to my pension fund and claimed tax relief on the rents paid while they were received tax-free. While the arrangement was very tax efficient, it fell down because the pension administrators saw it as an opportunity to charge excessive fees.

There are numerous ways to make tax savings and a myriad of tax pitfalls associated with business premises. I strongly advise that a tax adviser is consulted before the business premises are purchased.

Do You Need a Property Ownership Agreement?

Many areas of property ownership can lead to disputes when there is more than one proprietor involved, examples of which are as follows:

1. Disputes in respect of the valuation of the property upon changes in proprietors.
2. Disputes with new proprietors not wanting to take on shares of high fixed rate loans and early redemption penalty clauses.
3. Disputes regarding the costs of refurbishment expenditure near to a proprietor retiring.

4. Disputes regarding negative equity as a consequence of excessive development costs.
5. Disputes regarding the payment of a property share to a former proprietor.

In order to avoid these problem areas, business owners are strongly advised to have a property deed drafted to cover all matters that could relate to the property. The property deed should cover the procedures that will be adopted in the event of disputes.

An agreement is pretty standard, and most lawyers should be able to draft one for a modest fee.

How Do You Finance or Refinance the Property?

There will be occasions when a business owner will need to raise finance for the business, or for personal purposes. They can either provide the finance from their own resources or, as is more usual, approach the business bankers to ask them to provide the finance. The more usual situations where finance may be required are

1. Upon the purchase or construction of new premises.
2. Upon the retirement or appointment of a partner, where partners' shares in the business are transferred.
3. Upon the refinancing of the business premises to allow a drawdown of the partner's capital accounts (further in this chapter).
4. Upon the refinancing of the business premises to allow funding for further development of those premises.
5. Upon the transfer of the business borrowings to another lender to achieve savings from lower interest and bank charges.

When business owners approach a bank, they may be asked whether they would like a fixed or a variable loan.

A fixed rate loan is one where the interest rate charged for the entire period of the loan is fixed at the start, whereas a variable rate loan is one where the rate of interest changes when the official base rates change.

Although a fixed rate loan will give the business financial stability, in that the repayments on the loan will remain fixed for the whole of the repayment period (even though interest rates may rise), the business could lose out should the rate of interest fall.

The rates offered under fixed rate deals tend to be higher than the current variable rates, so they should only be considered if it is thought that rates will rise (the banker selling the fixed rate deal will always predict interest rate rises!).

There are other interest rate deals available, including capped rate deals, which offer the protection of a fixed rate arrangement, with the flexibility that the borrower can benefit from a reduction in interest rates (i.e., the interest charge is capped at an agreed amount and will not rise should interest rates increase).

With hindsight, it is easy to advise on fixed, capped or variable rate offers, but the instability of the financial markets means that it is always going to be a gamble.

Those that opt for fixed rate borrowings gain financial stability, but do they do it at a cost or a benefit? In truth, there is no correct answer to this query without resorting to a crystal ball.

Interest on a loan taken out for business purposes will attract tax relief. In order to maximize this tax relief, some businesses opt for an interest-only loan with the intention that they will pay off all personal, non-tax-efficient borrowings prior to the repayment of the capital on the business loan.

As well as maximizing the tax relief, this arrangement ensures that there is more cash to draw and, as long as the additional drawings are used to pay down personal borrowings or build up investments, this arrangement will benefit the borrowers.

Normally, over time the property loan will be paid down, and the value of the property will increase with the result that the net equity in the premises will increase, but this may not always be in the best interest of the business.

If the net equity is allowed to build up over the years, it may become a problem upon the retirement of a partner as

1. The business may have to take on additional borrowings to pay the partner out.
2. The cost of buying a share of the property to a new partner may be prohibitive.

Negative Equity and Valuations

Given the vagaries of the property market and the high level of borrowings taken on by a number of businesses, the possibility of a negative equity situation arising is very real.

This can also occur upon the construction of a purpose-built property, where the building value after completion can be worth less than the cost of construction.

In many cases, however, businesses, particularly those with a relatively high level of income and composed of principals not nearing retirement, will be able to weather this problem without too much difficulty.

They can wait for a few years with the reasonable expectation that property prices will increase over the medium term so that the negative equity will be extinguished.

In the interim, however, it may be difficult to attract new partners to the business, as bankers will be reluctant to lend (especially as new partners do not tend to have a high level of personal wealth to utilize as security).

The potential new partners could be indemnified by the existing ones to ensure that they do not incur a loss on a business failure.

Basis of Valuation

It is usual for each party to appoint their own professional valuer or surveyor to provide a valuation upon the sale or transfer of business premises.

The accepted basis for the valuation of business premises is that they are valued based on the continued use of the premises for their existing purpose.

However, there are instances where the premises may have a higher value for an alternative use.

It is important that any agreement between the business owners provides for differences in valuation and prescribes a course of action to prevent a dispute upon a change in principals.

Life Insurance and Endowments

Life insurance can be provided by various companies offering different policies, but the most common is term insurance. This is where the life of the policyholder is insured for a fixed amount in return for the payment of premiums over the term agreed.

The level of cover is dependent upon the health of the policyholder and the premiums that they are prepared to pay.

Most lenders will insist on borrowers taking out life insurance cover so that a business loan can be repaid upon their death.

This is understandable and quite straightforward when there is only one principal involved in the business. It gets complex, however, when there are multiple principals of different ages and with differing health issues, as the individual premiums may vary significantly.

This may be the cause of a dispute, as principals may be averse to subsidizing their colleagues. And some principals may already have significant personal cover that may be adequate for security purposes.

To prevent a dispute, it is usual that the principals are charged with the cost of their own premiums.

Where life insurance is taken out, the documentation needs to be checked to ensure that the beneficiaries are those with an interest in paying off the loan, and also that the insurance cover is flexible enough to provide for the reduction in the borrowing as it is repaid.

I have come across disputes where a principal of a business has died and his widow has received the life insurance proceeds in error, leaving his partners to pay off his share of the borrowings.

I have also found a business paying for term insurance against a repayment loan, which resulted in an excess on the death of a partner. This resulted in tax problems regarding the excess, and a dispute as to the payment of that excess to the widow.

Endowments are life insurance policies that have an investment element within them, in that the beneficiary receives a return at the end of the insurance term. There are specific tax rules regarding these policies.

They are not as popular as they used to be as the investment returns have decreased from the highs received in the late 1990s, and those wishing an investment return can find better financial products elsewhere.

Business owners who do not cover their borrowings with sufficient life insurance are gambling with the future of their families and employees, as an uninsured business is likely to fold upon the death of the principal.

It is essential that business owners use financial advisers with experience in their industry, as there have been many instances of inappropriate policies being sold. A testament to this are the mis-selling scandals that have nearly bankrupted a number of banks in recent years.

Critical Illness and Health Insurance

As covered in the What Should You Do To Protect Your Income section, it is important that a business takes out insurance to protect itself from key personnel falling ill. It is also important that those personnel protect themselves against their personal loss of income should their illness be serious.

The financial risks of a serious illness to the business and the individual are high as a study by the American Association for Critical Illness Insurance has found. A 25-year-old, non-smoker has a 24% chance of having a critical illness (i.e., cancer, heart attack or stroke) prior to reaching the age of 65. The odds on that individual increase to 49% if he is a smoker.

The cost of illness can be significant, with nearly two-thirds of US bankruptcies a result of medical expenses.

But how should the costs of insuring against illness be borne? The company should insure itself for the loss of income, and pay this cost itself?

The cost of private medical insurance policies of key personnel can be paid personally or (if incorporated) paid by the company as part of their remuneration package.

Next, we will look at the difference in the net cost of the employee and the company paying for private medical insurance.

1. If the employee pays the premium personally there is no benefit-in-kind, but the cost is met from income that has already been taxed.

For example, a premium of £1000 paid personally out of dividend income, which had been subject to tax of 32.5%, the employee would need to receive gross dividends of £1481.

And, as dividends are paid from the company's net profits after tax, the profits needed to pay that dividend would need to be £1851.25.

2. If the company pays the premium on the employee's behalf, it is treated as a business expense and a taxable benefit-in-kind. Tax of 40% is payable on this benefit-in-kind.

The company will have to pay 13.8% national insurance on the payment, bringing the total cost allowable against corporation tax to £1138.

This total cost of £1138 will attract tax relief of £227.60, bringing the net cost of the premium payment to £910.40.

As there will be tax of £400 to pay on the benefit-in-kind, a gross dividend of £670 would need to be paid to allow for this.

The profits needed to allow this dividend payment would be £837.50. When this amount is added to the net cost of paying the premium of £910.40, a profit of £1747.90 would be needed to pay the premium.

This represents a saving of £103.35, which on the face of it is very small, but if you were formulating a policy of how the medical insurance premiums of 200 staff should be paid, the total savings would be £20,670.00!

Please note how such a minor matter can have a significant effect on the profit. We will look at this further in Chapter 9.

Fixtures and Equipment

The fixtures and equipment usually found in a business can be broken down into the following categories:

1. Furniture such as desks, chairs, filing cabinets, bookcases, cupboards and some floor coverings.
2. Specialist equipment for the specific business, for example, dental chairs.
3. Office equipment such as computers, printers, telephones and cash registers.
4. Sundry other equipment such as vacuum cleaners, tea- and coffee-making facilities, pictures and equipment to provide background music.
5. Items of plant which are integral to the building, such as fitted cupboards and ambient lighting systems.

These items will be shown in the accounts at their purchase cost less a provision for depreciation to write off that cost over the estimated useful life of those assets.

When a business is sold, it is usual to have the fixtures and equipment valued, and that value used as the purchase price for the new owner.

Tax allowances are available to reflect the loss in value of these assets over their estimated useful lives, with the allowance claimable dependent upon the type of asset and the date it was purchased.

Different options as to the financing of these assets can be found later in this chapter.

Motor Vehicles

This category of assets within the accounts usually comprises the proprietor's own cars, pool cars and commercial vehicles.

This category usually represents those vehicles owned by the business, and not those on lease. Leasing of vehicles has become a very popular way for businesses to meet their transport needs.

This is as a result of the vehicle manufacturers discovering that this method of financing vehicles encourages more frequent renewal of stock by customers.

The finance packages currently offered to businesses, and frequently to individuals, allow the customer to, effectively, hire and use the vehicle for a fixed period, and run it for a pre-agreed mileage.

There is an agreed future value assessed on the vehicle, based on the age and mileage, and the hirer is obliged to return the vehicle at the end of the period. A penalty is charged for excess mileage.

At the end of the period, the customer often replaces the vehicle with a new one on the same terms, and the manufacturer (or its retailer) can sell the original vehicle on the secondhand market.

The benefit to the manufacturer of these arrangements is that there is a continued demand for their vehicles.

The benefits to the customer are

1. They only pay for the depreciation of the vehicle over the period of ownership, often at a cost in line with the cost of purchase.
2. They can upgrade their vehicle on a regular basis.

The alternative to the leasing model is for the business to buy the vehicles by way of loan.

This can sometimes result in the value of the vehicle being less than the borrowings on it.

The allowances that can be claimed against business income on vehicles used by the business are covered in Chapter 6.

Current Assets

As previously mentioned, current assets usually comprise stock, debtors, cash and bank accounts, which can be described as liquid assets as they represent cash or items that can be quickly converted to cash.

Stock

A business needs to hold a stock of the goods that it sells so that it is able to satisfy demand for goods in a reasonable time frame.

The amount of stock held by a business can vary significantly depending upon the business's internal procedures and the ability of suppliers to supply the business on a shorter time cycle.

There are two conflicting aims when it comes to buying stock for a business. The first aim is to hold as little stock as possible, as that stock represents the proprietor's money that is tied up in the business.

The other aim is to buy stock as cheaply as possible, but as that often results in having to buy in bulk, the level of stock rises. Most businesses find a happy medium.

The cardinal rule is to have sufficient stock to deal with demand, and never to miss a sale due to lack of stock to sell.

Where significant stocks are held, a proper stocktake should take place at least once a year, and that valuation should be included within the accounts. Most businesses should be operating a computerized stock system, and the stocktake is a chance to measure the accuracy of that system and the stock levels it is disclosing.

There are other benefits to operating a stock system, which include identifying whether staff are recording (and charging) sales correctly and identifying any thefts.

If a business does not perform a stocktake, it may include an estimate of the amount of stock it holds on its balance sheet. If the estimate is for a round sum amount, it could lead to an inquiry into the accounts from the Tax Authorities, who expect accurate figures from businesses. While they do accept estimates from small businesses, they do expect better records from larger businesses.

A detailed stocktake would take place upon the sale or transfer of the whole or part of a business. For the retiring proprietor, this ensures that they are receiving their share of value, while the continuing business owners can take the opportunity to identify obsolete and outdated stock.

There is an art to the selection of the stocks purchased for resale, especially in the retail sector, where the impulse buy by the customer can provide a significant proportion of sales income. In these instances, if the staff can be rewarded for encouraging the sale of high-value items, the profits can be improved significantly.

Debtors

Business accounts need to be drafted on an earnings basis, and not merely to show receipts and payments during the accounting year. Therefore, at the year-end, an account needs to be taken of all outstanding items that remain due, but unpaid.

The debtors of a business represent the amounts that are owed to the business at any time, and most accounting software will produce those figures for the business when required. It is important that the business is able to determine the amounts due to it, so that it can chase up its debts. Most businesses do this on a monthly basis.

Producing a list of amounts due to the business on a regular basis will help to identify those amounts which remain long overdue, otherwise known as bad debts.

The production of this list is the responsibility of the credit controller, which is a key position within a business.

Businesses can also utilize the services of debt management companies to chase debts and help get their finances in order. To commence an action to collect a debt, it is essential that the company has the documentation in place to substantiate the debt, so it is important that adequate records are kept of sales, and payments thereof.

Many businesses accept credit card and mobile payments when selling their goods, and pay a fee to the credit card provider for that facility. The amount varies from bank to bank, and the costs can accumulate to a substantial amount.

This is why some businesses refuse to accept credit card payments for amounts below a de minimis level.

Accepting payments by credit card reduces the chances of bad debts and increases the market that the business is selling to, as a large number of customers will not buy from businesses that do not accept credit cards (up to 69% of millennials say they will not deal with businesses that do not accept credit cards).

Credit Card Facilities

Businesses wishing to provide credit/debit card facilities will incur the following costs:

1. Setup fees for merchant accounts: These fees can be anywhere between £40 and £160.
2. Credit card processing and transaction fees: These typically fall between 2% and 3% per transaction, but they can get as high as 4% for international transactions (which may or may not include a currency conversion fee).
3. Implementation costs for setting up equipment, such as point-of-sale (POS) terminals.
4. Customer charge fees if the purchaser decides to dispute a credit card transaction.
5. Fraud accountability: Some banks and credit card issuers may hold the business liable if fraudsters charge and receive products and services using stolen customer data.

Despite the costs of providing better payment facilities, businesses that don't offer credit card facilities will not prosper.

With card and mobile payments likely to increase significantly over the next decade, implementing the systems to accept card payments is essential, as estimates have been made that only up to 23% of sales will have been in cash by the end of 2017.

Customers are more likely to undertake impulse buys if they can use a credit card/mobile payment, and there is less need for people to hold cash as more businesses are welcoming new methods of payments, such as Applepay.

The acceptance of credit/debit/mobile payments has resulted in safer money handling practices, as the time and expense of counting, sorting and transporting cash are reduced.

Additionally, holding less cash on the premises can make businesses less attractive to thieves, and in theory cheaper to insure!

New technology is increasing the security of credit transactions and decreasing the risk of fraud.

Credit cards have evolved into one of the most common methods of consumer payment, with nearly 60% of US consumers preferring cards over cash.

Debtors (Work in Progress and Prepayments)

Included within the debtors' figure on the business balance sheet earlier in this chapter, there may also be work in progress to account for. This is when work has been undertaken on behalf of a customer, but it has not yet reached the stage where it can be invoiced. The work in progress provision is to ensure that the costs involved in this work are accounted for in the same period as the invoice.

Other forms of debtors that need accounting for are prepayments. These occur where expenses have been paid in advance, such as yearly insurance premiums. The advance payment is calculated and shown in the accounts as a prepayment, with the amount being carried forward.

Cash at Bank and in Hand

The figures included on a business balance sheet for cash at bank represent the reconciled balances at the year-end. The reconciled current account bank balance in the business records rarely matches the actual amount on the bank statement, as the former represents the balance in the bank account at the year-end date, less the checks written out and not presented at that date, plus the receipts banked but not yet cleared.

Usually, a small amount of cash will be included on the balance sheet, this amount representing unbanked sales, the money held in cash registers and petty cash.

Petty cash will normally be held to fund trivial bills such as coffee, tea, newspapers, window cleaning, etc.

Those businesses which build up cash surpluses in deposit accounts will also show these amounts in this category on the balance sheet.

Current Liabilities

The liabilities of a business represent the amounts that the business owes to others, and are usually split in the accounts (especially in company accounts, where it is a legal require-ment) between current and long-term liabilities.

Current liabilities are those that are due for payment within 12 months, and long-term liabilities represent those amounts due thereafter.

Current liabilities are usually those amounts due to suppli-ers, or bills for expenses, where it is usual to be given 30 days credit.

Also within the category of current liabilities are 'accruals'. These are expenses that have been incurred by the business for which an invoice has not yet been raised. The accountancy bill for dealing with the year-end submissions etc. would be an example of an accrual, as the invoice is usually raised after all the procedures have been completed, which is often after the year-end itself.

A bank overdraft is another example of a current liability, as this is usually repayable upon demand.

If the business is incorporated, making profits and provid-ing employment, it will create liabilities for both PAYE and corporate taxes. These would normally be provided in the accounts as current liabilities at the year-end date.

Balances due within 1 year on loans and finance arrange-ments would also be included as current liabilities. The bal-ances due after 12 months would be shown as long-term liabilities (see section below).

Where businesses are incorporated, the transactions between the proprietor and his or her company would nor-mally be recorded in a 'director's loan account' and included within current liabilities. Examples of such transactions are

■ Capital introduced from own resources or financed by personal borrowings.

- Amounts drawn from the business, usually in lieu of dividends declared.
- Company expenses funded personally by the proprietor.
- Personal expenses of the proprietor funded by the company.

It would be usual to find the director's loan account in creditors, reflecting the fact that the company owed the director for funds introduced to the company. If it is found as a debtor, it means that the director has taken excess funds from the company and may be subject to a tax charge on the amount.

Long-Term Liabilities

Often, the long-term liabilities of a business consist wholly of balances due on loans and finance arrangements.

Given the cost of buying stock for resale and the finances needed for ongoing expenses, a business requires a level of money to operate, known as working capital.

Often, this funding requirement is resolved by way of a loan.

In addition, funds may have been required to buy the business and to renovate the business premises to a reasonable standard. This funding is often provided by way of bank borrowing, either an overdraft or a loan.

A loan will be disclosed within the accounts, and the element within long-term liabilities will represent that part of the loan which is due for repayment after 1 year.

The purchase of equipment is often funded by finance agreements that can be taken out over a period of years, usually three to five.

From the repayment schedule, it is possible to identify the amounts that will be due within, and after, 1 year, and disclose those amounts in the accounts as appropriate.

If the amount of borrowing is significant, it is normal for the lender to ask the borrower for some form of security or guarantee, and proprietors often sign personal guarantees to secure their business borrowings.

These guarantees will give the banks access to the proprietor's personal assets should the loan not be repaid within the agreed timetable.

Purchase of Assets and Equipment: Cash, Hire Purchase or Lease?

What is the best way to finance the purchase of new assets? In most cases, if cash is available, it is preferable to use that to buy the asset outright, although this may tie up limited cash resources.

The interest on a loan will often be more than the return the cash would receive on deposit, so it is better to use that cash, if no better use for it can be foreseen. Those setting up in business for the first time will have limited cash flow, and it is often preferable to spread the payments over a period of time. But is it better to buy an asset on hire purchase, with a loan or lease it?

The following paragraphs summarize the differences in the way assets are treated when they are financed by different methods.

Purchase with own cash: If proprietors use their own funds to buy the asset, they will own that asset from the outset, and be able to get tax relief on the cost in the year of purchase (and later years).

Purchase with an unsecured loan: Again, the proprietor will own the asset from the outset and be able to claim tax relief on the cost in the year of purchase (and later years). (An unsecured loan is one given by a lender free of any security. A secured loan would give the lender a security over the asset being purchased, or other assets of the borrower.)

Given that the lender is in a safer position with a secured loan, the rates charged on those loans are usually less than those on unsecured loans.

Purchase under a hire purchase agreement: Under a hire purchase agreement, the proprietors are treated as owning the asset from the outset, but legal ownership only passes to them on the payment of the final 'option to purchase' fee. Again, the full cost gets tax relief in the year of purchase (and later years). Usually, a hire purchase loan is secured on the asset to which it relates.

Purchase by way of a lease: Under this arrangement, the leasing company owns the asset for the period of the lease, and the periodic leasing payments attract tax relief, as they are paid, through the profit and loss account. Often, at the end of the initial lease period (usually 3–5 years), a secondary lease period will commence with the asset being leased to the business at a peppercorn rent in perpetuity, effectively giving the business ownership of the asset.

In order to strengthen the finance market, and to create ways to circumvent the tax regulations, financial institutions have invented hybrid finance arrangements under a myriad of names, which effectively provide the same financial benefits as above.

When an asset is bought, tax relief can usually be obtained in the year of purchase (and later years). If the asset is leased, tax relief can be obtained only over the period of the lease.

The following schedule explains the tax relief in detail:

JT's Restaurant is planning to purchase a kitchen range for £10,000. The options it has been given are (1) to buy using available cash; (2) to lease over a period of 3 years at a cost of £320/month; or (3) to purchase using a loan of £10,000 repayable by 36 monthly payments of £320.22 (at 9.9% APR).

Under option (1), the tax allowances of 18% of the written-down cost can be claimed each year (on a reducing balance basis).

Year 1 Cost	£10,000
Capital allowance claim	(£1,800)
Net value c/f to year 2	£8,200
Capital allowance claim	(£1,476)
Net value c/f to year 3	£6,724
Capital allowance claim	(£1,210)
Net value c/f to year 4	£5,514

Total allowances of £4,486.

Under option (2), the cost of the lease payments can be offset against income each year; therefore, £3840 of lease costs would be allowed as an expense against income in each of the 3 years. A total of £11,520.

Under option (3), the capital allowances of £4486 would be allowable, but in addition the interest on the loan (of £1,527.92) would be allowable as an expense. A total of £6,013.92.

The interest has been calculated as follows:

Total loan amount	£10,000.00
Total amount of repayments	
£320.22×36	£11,527.92
Difference (interest charge)	£1,527.92

On the face of it, the leasing option looks the best until you consider that the ownership of the range is still with the leasing company, unless a peppercorn agreement is taken to obtain ownership in perpetuity.

Also under options (1) and (3), there is still £5514 of costs to be claimed in capital allowances in future years.

Annual Percentage Rate

Given how inconclusive the previous example is, it may be time to look at the Annual Percentage Rate (APR), as the APR is often hidden within the lease agreement paperwork, making it difficult to compare the cost of a loan and/or lease against a lease.

APR is a tool for understanding the cost of borrowing, whether it's a loan, a credit card or a mortgage. Although APR is not perfect, it gives you a standard for comparing interest and fees from different lenders.

The official definition of APR is the yearly interest payable on the amount borrowed plus any other applicable charges, all expressed as an annual rate charge.

As the APR includes fees, not just interest charges, it gives a better understanding of the costs of finance.

In other words, it is the interest and expenses that you pay when you take a loan and repay it. For example, if you borrow £100 and the loan APR you are given is 56%, you would pay back £156 in total in the year you borrowed it.

APR allows you to evaluate the cost of the loan in terms of a percentage. If your loan has a 10% rate, you'll pay £10 per £100 you borrow annually.

All other things being equal, you simply want the loan with the lowest APR.

If you are considering leasing or buying business equipment, it is usual to look at the available options in some detail. At this stage, it would be helpful to know how to calculate the APR on a leasing deal.

In order to calculate the APR on a leasing agreement, you need to know:

1. The capital value of the equipment
2. The term over which you wish to lease and the lease details
3. The lease rental payment

The following example will show how the APR can be calculated:

- The equipment being acquired is a kitchen range with a Capital Cost of £10,000.00
- The lease rental agreement is based on 36 monthly repayments with 1 month payable on delivery
- The quoted lease rental payment is £320.00 per month

The total rental repayments come to £11,520.00, comprising the Capital Cost of £10,000 plus an additional cost of notional interest of £1,520.

Working Out the Leasing Deal APR

The first step is to work out what the flat rate interest is on your deal. To do this, you simply divide the total interest payable by the number of years. In our example:

- Interest of £1,520.00 over 3 years equals £506.70 per year.
- Divide this annual figure of £506.70 by the Capital Cost of your equipment; in this case £10,000. This gives you a flat interest rate of just over 5.067%.
- The APR is roughly twice the flat rate, hence the APR in our example is 10.134%.

The reason for the simplistic/rough approach is the complexity of compound interest and the reduction in the balance as it is paid off. This makes an exact calculation very difficult.

This complexity can be seen in the following table:

A business has been offered a 5-year loan for £100,000 at a rate of 10%, with the total amount being repayable at the end of the 5 years.

The business has been offered the loan on a simple interest or a compound interest basis, which one should it accept?

	Simple Interest		Compound Interest	
	Interest Amount	Amount to Repay	Interest Amount	Amount to Repay
Principal		£100,000		£100,000
Year one	£10,000	£110,000	£10,000	£110,000
Year two	£10,000	£120,000	£11,000	£121,000
Year three	£10,000	£130,000	£12,100	£133,100
Year four	£10,000	£140,000	£13,310	£146,410
Year five	£10,000	£150,000	£14,641	£161,051

Compound interest reflects the interest on the principal as it changes each year. The complexity with compound interest loans is that the interest is charged on the principal as the repayments are being made. It is, as they say, a moveable feast. As you can see from the table, interest is charged on interest.

The above shows why it is difficult to calculate the APR without some very serious mathematics. The following is the equation for calculating an accurate APR:

$$\sum_{K=1}^{K=m} \frac{A_K}{(1+i)^{t_K}} = \sum_{K'=1}^{K'=m'} \frac{A'_{K'}}{(1+i)^{t_{K'}}}$$

where:

K is the number identifying a particular advance of credit
K' is the number identifying a particular instalment
A_K is the amount of advance K
A'_K is the amount of instalment K'
Σ represents the sum of all terms indicated

m is the number of advances of credit

m' is the total number of instalments

t_K is the interval, expressed in years, between the *relevant date* and the date of the second advance and those of any subsequent advances numbers three to m

t_K' is the interval, expressed in years, between the *relevant date* and the dates of instalments numbered one to m'

This formula has been reproduced from the FCA.org.UK handbook.

Excessive APRs on Payday Loans

Payday loans are very expensive, but on the face of it appear cheap. These loans are often marketed as interest-free or low-interest rate loans, but the fees make them problematic. But even the fees are 'sold' as minimal, and when you look at them in terms of APR, there are much better ways to borrow money.

Take, for example, if you were to apply for an interest-free payday loan for £500, on which a fee of £50 is charged. The loan is only needed for 14 days. The APR on this loan can be calculated as follows:

1. Divide the fee by the loan amount.
2. Multiply the amount by 365 (days).
3. Divide the result by the term of the loan (in days).
4. Multiply the result by 100.

If the preceding loan details are processed:

1. £50 divided by £500 is 0.01.
2. 0.01 multiplied by 365 is 36.5.
3. 36.5 divided by 14 is 2.6071.
4. 2.6071 multiplied by 100 is 260.71 (this is the APR in decimal format).

Given that it is that difficult to calculate an exact APR, many loans are marketed using an estimate of what the APR will be, called the 'representative APR', which may not reflect the actual APR so the borrower needs to be wary of additional charges etc. that may be added to the loan after the initial agreement has been taken.

Credit card providers advertise an APR based on the interest rates they charge, but this does not include the effect of compounding, and the actual amount paid is almost always more than that quoted.

The APR paid by those who only make small or minimum payments against their credit card liability can be very high, as they will be paying interest on interest.

Credit card providers do not have to include their charges in their APR, only the interest costs. This means that their annual fees, balance transfer fees and other charges will have a significant impact on the APR, with the borrower being unaware of the true cost of their borrowing.

The sad fact is that those with the least, who are forced to borrow on credit cards and payday loans, are exploited by financial institutions. The fat cat, with the morality of a piece of wood, may call it market forces and wash his hands of the problem.

Which begs the question: do 21st-century financiers have a responsibility to use their skills and resources for the good? Have the days of greed gone?

From the evidence coming from current business practice, with the increase in child employment, the exploitation of third-world resources and questionable employment practices, I think not!

But enough of my socialist views, and let's return to the topic of APRs.

The rules regarding the sales of some mortgages demand that the APR on a mortgage includes the fees and charges as well as the interest. The quotes provided by mortgage companies might or might not include other costs incurred to get the loan approved (such as insurances).

Lenders are able to choose what they include in their APR calculations, so it is important to look closely at what is included when comparing loans.

The ability of the borrower to pay the charges early can also have an impact on the loan's APR.

The foregoing information shows that there are a number of matters that need reviewing when comparing loans and leases, and there is no universal right answer to financing assets.

Net Assets

This figure should represent the net worth of the business at the balance sheet date. In the example balance sheet, the net asset value is £498,000, and this is the amount, in theory, that would be generated by the sale of the business. So, if the goodwill and fixed assets were sold for £700,000, the stock sold, the debtors monies collected and the funds utilized in paying off the debts, including loans, the amount left in the bank would be £498,000.

This is a theoretical exercise, as the amount collected would depend upon whether the values on the balance sheet were up to date and actually achieved upon a sale.

However, the balance sheet is a good indicator of a business's worth, and can be brought up to date quite easily by obtaining current valuations in the event of the sale of whole or part of the business.

Remember, this is the value that you are building up to retire with.

Funding of Business Accounts

One aspect of business accounts that is often queried by entrepreneurs is that of capital. How does capital accumulate, how is it distributed between the principals and why can it not be drawn out?

These are the more common questions asked on this topic, along with the matters of (1) the introduction of the capital into the business, (2) how it is described in the accounts and (3) by what means should it be contributed to by an incoming partner.

Most of the following details apply to partnerships, but once the concepts are understood they can easily be applied to all business formats.

If the capital in a business is managed correctly, it can assist the principals in future planning and in some cases present significant tax advantages.

The capital of the majority of businesses can be fairly easily allocated to the following three headings:

Property capital: This usually represents the proprietors' interest in the equity in the business premises and, in some cases, the fixed assets of the business. This is often separately identified in the accounts as the 'capital accounts' of those principals with an interest in those assets. As this capital is represented by physical assets, it cannot easily be withdrawn from the business.

Other (or fixed asset) capital: This represents the principals' interest in the non-building fixed assets of the business, i.e., the fixtures and fittings, office equipment, computers, etc. These are assets from which the principals earn their income, and would normally be owned in the same proportions as those in which the principals would share the business income and expense.

However, a number of businesses operate a system whereby each principal owns their equipment personally: in these cases, the costs need to be attributed to the principals and shown as separate 'capital' accordingly.

Working capital: This represents the funds needed to finance the day-to-day operation of the business, and is often called the 'current account'. This amount is usually made up by the net investment in the practice assets as follows:

Stocks for resale and consumables
Amounts owed to the business
Work in progress and uninvoiced work
Cash and bank balances
Amounts owed by the business

Although the capital has been broken down into the above three headings, it is more usual to see it broken down into two headings in most partnership accounts, more usually known as the 'capital' and the 'current' account.

Capital Accounts

Although there are no set rules as to which assets are financed by a principal's capital and current accounts, it is usual to see the net equity in the premises reflected by the capital account, with the balance of the business finance being funded by the current account.

The capital and current accounts are often held in equal shares by the partners, or in line with the percentage of the business profits they will receive.

In the example balance sheet, the capital accounts of the principals would represent the costs of the property and all other fixed assets less the balance on the property loans, as follows:

Fixed assets	700,000
Loans	(235,000)
Capital account	465,000

Capital accounts are often based on the cost of the property on the balance sheet, and this cost is often an accumulation of the expense on the property over a number of years. It is important to regularly review the cost of the property against an estimation of its actual value, for the following reasons:

1. If the market value is less than the accumulated costs in the accounts, there is a negative equity situation and the principals would need to reflect the loss in value by reducing their capital account balances.

    This can happen when there are construction costs on the property, and those costs are in excess of the added value to the property.
2. If the market value is in excess of the costs in the accounts, the equity position needs to be discussed, so that all principals are aware that they would need to provide the business with more funds to buy another principal out.
3. It is often useful to provide the business bankers with accounts that show the property at its current market value, so that they can assess the loan-to-value ratio on any funding secured on the property.

The business could renegotiate the terms of its loans if the value of the net equity in the property has increased significantly.

Current Accounts

Current accounts reflect the amounts that the principals initially introduced to the business, as well as their accumulated undrawn profits of the business to date, and this provides the funding for the working capital of the business.

The principal's profit share will be posted to his/her current account, plus any monies he/she has introduced to the business. Amounts in respect of his/her drawings and liabilities paid on his/her behalf are then deducted from the current account.

An increase in the current account balance in the year reflects the underdrawing of a principal's profits. Likewise, a decrease would reflect an overdrawing.

The following is an example of a simple current account:

	£
Amount introduced to the business	10,000
Profit share for the year	35,000
Amounts drawn in the year	(27,000)
Balance	18,000

An understanding of how a current account is calculated is important for those wishing to take control of their business finances.

To encourage good working capital management, businesses should work to an agreed level of current account (i.e., agree to the level of funds that the principals should tie up in the business). This level should be sufficient to provide for cash that the business needs to operate, plus to provide for any future planned increases in fixed assets. It is important for the business to set this figure as it represents a target to aim for, and to ensure that excesses do not build up in the business that could otherwise be drawn.

Without detailed accounts being prepared on a regular basis, it is quite easy for the partners' current accounts to get out of balance, and in equal share partnerships disputes can arise as to 'who is financing who' when the differences are significant.

Drawings and the Payment of Tax

The calculation of the principal's withdrawals (drawings) from a business is a relatively simple operation when budgets are being drafted. The drawings should reflect the forecast profit.

If excess funds are building up in the bank account, it means that the budgeted profit is being exceeded.

Calculation of the drawings needs to take into account whether the business is also paying the proprietor's tax from the profits.

It is important that the current accounts are being monitored in partnerships where the partners enjoy different shares of the business profit.

Where a business has agreed to pay the partners' tax, calculation of the drawings is complicated, as it is unusual for each principal to have the same tax bill.

Where the partners have to account for their own tax bills, the business can pay equal drawings to each principal enjoying the same profit share.

It is important each year for the principals to review their individual current accounts as often differences in tax bills and bookkeeping errors can result in the partner's capital accounts getting out of balance.

There are often disagreements between partners in a business and their accountants, when differences in the balances on their current accounts are pointed out, especially when they have overdrawn their profits and need to input funds into the business.

Accountants

Following on from the previous mention of the accountant, it may be time to discuss the appointment of one. An accountant is a key professional who can be a focal member of your team, and guide you in the running of your business… but how do you decide which one to pick?

How Do You Find a Good Accountant?

Accountancy is one of the few professions where people can practice without having any type of qualification. Anyone can open an office and tell the world that they are the best accountant in the world. So, how do you ensure that the accountant you pick to deal with your personal and business affairs has sufficient knowledge of your business sector and the tax legislation that is relevant to your income?

The following suggestions should help in the selection of an accountant who is knowledgeable in your business sector.

■ Ask your competitors and other businesses in the same sector who their accountants are and whether they would recommend them to you; although this will not always ensure that the accountant is knowledgeable, as that business owner may not be aware of the better services being offered by other accountants, it at least shows that the accountant has sufficient skills to be recommended to you by his client.

■ Look in the trade press at both the advertisements in the classified section and also in the body of the magazine for any finance or taxation articles written by accountants specifically for your business sector.

■ Look on the websites of the *Institute of Chartered Accountants in England and Wales* (ICAEW: www.icaew.com) and the Association of Certified Accountants (ACCA: www.accaglobal.com) in the UK, or your local Certified Public Accountants Institute (www.aicpa.org) in the USA and worldwide, for the members nearest to you. These associations have strict membership criteria and usually demand that members hold professional negligence insurance, which will ensure some type of recourse should the service be failing in any way.

The benefit of appointing an accountant who specializes in your business sector is that they can advise on the following:

Benchmarking: With details of many businesses in the same sector, they are able to advise on the level of business profits, and where efficiencies and cost savings can be made.

Goodwill: The accountant should have details of a number of business sales in that sector and they can ascertain whether the value attributable to the goodwill you are being charged, or are going to charge, is reasonable.

Incorporation: They can advise on the tax planning, structural planning and pension issues involved in the incorporation process and can highlight issues with income protection, associated companies and VAT.

Business Sale or Purchase: They can advise on the sale or purchase of a business and assist in the raising of finance, and have a detailed knowledge of bank lending parameters.

In addition to the above, most specialist accountants can provide advice on strategy and profit improvement and provide valuations for lending purposes.

What Should You Expect from Your Accountant?

Non-specialist accountants often supply their business clients with a standard set of accounts and a completed tax return, but provide very little else within their service. This is often as a result of a lack of knowledge of the business sector.

Businesses should expect more than merely a set of account and a tax return; they should be provided with an interpretation of their results that will provide them with a high level of management information and advice. This is not something that accountants offering online services are capable of doing.

Your accountant should take an active role in the growth of your business, bringing to you the tips for success he has learned from his more successful clients. He has a vested interest in encouraging the growth of your business, as the bigger you get, the higher the fees he can charge.

Accountants tend to devote more of their time to their larger clients, as these clients' needs for regular advice increase.

Legal Advisors

As previously discussed, a lot of the processes of running a business require the input of a legal advisor, and it is vital that a business appoints one that is competent.

Legal disputes can be very costly but can be avoided by getting things right in the first place. A good lawyer can ensure this happens.

Solicitors, How Do You Find a Good One?

The answer to this is very similar to that for accountants, in that you should look for an advisor who is knowledgeable of your industry and able to provide more than a basic legal service.

What Should You Expect from Your Solicitor?

A specialist advisor should already have experience of dealing with disputes specific to the industry and should provide advice on to how to avoid them.

They should also be able to provide draft documentation that takes into account the disputes that have arisen in the past. For example, property disputes within partnerships can be avoided by providing for them in the partnership agreement.

The Annual Review Meeting

It is important that a business takes time out to review its performance and plan for the future. This should be done on a regular basis, at least annually.

The meeting should take place away from the distractions of running the business on a day-to-day basis to ensure that those concerned can give the process their full attention.

My firm booked a nice hotel in the Lake District for
a weekend away each year, at a slack time of the year.
The review should include:

1. Review of annual accounts
2. Review of forecasts against actual
3. Preparation of forecasts for next year to include changes
   in wages, drawings, etc.
4. Plans for capital investment/mergers/acquisitions, etc.
5. Discuss the appointment of legal/accountancy advisors

Chapter 8

Promoting Your Business

The task of marketing your small business may seem daunting, but it is easy to let the world know that you are there.

It doesn't cost a fortune to run a successful publicity program, and I include a few helpful ideas in this chapter.

Successful marketing can include a variety of tactics, and it is important that you use more than one in your efforts to communicate with your potential customers.

Your customers may become resistant to a single approach, and its effectiveness may wane in time.

You need to consider a number of different ways to contact customers, for example, letters, classified advertising, social media, leafleting, etc. Spend a lot of time making your website the best, which may involve utilizing the services of professional website designers.

The Business Website

Your website is your virtual shop window and your chance to promote your services and products to generate online sales.

Concentrate on making your website customer focused and simple to navigate, so that their time on the site is minimized. All you need from them is

1. A sale.
2. The customer to click onto a link which generates income for the business.
3. Their details for future marketing purposes.
4. Their details to sell on to another for marketing purposes.

A website is a 24/7 sales tool and is key to a business's success. The following areas should be focused on to maximize the website's value:

- The website should be easy to use and informative so that a customer can easily discover details of your product or service and buy without a problem.
- The web designer should think like your customer and gear the website experience to the customer's needs. Both the website designer and yourself need to research the target audience and their needs first.
- The goal of the website needs to be set first. Is it to be used for e-commerce (i.e., will it be a direct sales portal) or is its purpose to inform new customers or to provide a service to existing customers?
- Keep it simple and easy for all browsers to load.
- Make a note of bad websites you come across, what's bad and what shouldn't you do?
- Be open to feedback from your customers regarding their experience on the website.
- Be unique and use humor to get your message across.
- Remember that the latest is not necessarily the best; use tried and tested methods if they do the job.
- Reviewing your new or existing website and improving it to match your target customer will prove a smart investment for your business.

■ Continually review your website and sales statistics to assess its effectiveness, and update if necessary.

Return on Investment

Expenditure on a website is an investment in the business, and this seems as good a time as any to explore the concept of 'return on investment'.

The return on investment is a method of measuring how much a business can benefit from its expenditure on a project.

For example, if a business is considering purchasing its own van to reduce its mailing costs of £5,000 a year, it needs to consider whether the costs of doing so would produce a saving.

The van, driver, fuel and other costs are estimated to be, initially £10,000 and £2,000 a year thereafter. The return on investment can be calculated as follows:

	Year One	Year Two	Year Three	Year Four	Total
Investment in van and costs	£10,000	£2,000	£2,000	£2,000	£16,000
Mailing costs saved	£5,000	£5,000	£5,000	£5,000	£20,000
Return/surplus	(£5,000)	£3,000	£3,000	£3,000	£4,000

The business is forecast to make a saving of £4,000 over a 4-year period, and £3,000 a year thereafter. This is the return on investment.

In the foregoing example, it is fairly easy to calculate the return on investment, but it is not quite so clear when the expenditure is on something like a website, as the additional income it will generate is hard to identify.

In order to quantify the benefit of a project, such as the expense of a website, it is necessary to identify the goals that the project is going to achieve. In the case of a website, it will be

1. An increase in the targeted traffic to the site.
2. An increase in the sales and/or leads.
3. An increase in the positive feedback from visitors to the site.
4. An increase in the website traffic converting to an increase in sales.
5. An increase in the checkout rate (are people completing the sale or abandoning the shopping cart?).

In order to do this, a process to monitor the targets needs to be created, so that the return on the expenditure can be assessed.

Numerous apps are available that monitor traffic to a website and the behavior of those browsing. I recommend that you invest in this technology.

Mailings

Produce a professional-looking flyer or brochure and enclose it with all the outgoing mail, to reduce the mailing costs of a separate mailing.

Although these items are often discarded by their recipients, those who don't will have something tangible that they can refer back to should they consider they need your services in the future.

Produce a newsletter to send to existing customers, business referrers and potential customers. This can either be mailed or e-mailed, and should be used to encourage brand support.

Encourage visitors to your website to subscribe to your e-mail newsletters.

E-mail Campaigns

It is cheaper to send a large number of e-mails as part of a marketing plan, than it is to actually mail the recipients. But, is it an effective way of contacting your customers?

According to a survey by Campaign Monitor in 2015, for every $1 invested, e-mail marketing generates an average return of $38.

Detailed analysis can be provided of the results of an e-mail campaign, which show the number of e-mails that were opened, how many were then clicked through to the website and how many resulted in the intended sale.

Therefore, we are likely to see e-mail marketing used more by businesses in the future.

With all the advances in marketing technology, it is still surprising to see businesses that have failed to modernize and waste money on ineffectual marketing campaigns.

If, after reading this, you still think that an advert in the newsagent's window will be enough, you've missed the point, as it is easier than ever to attract customers to your business. Unfortunately, it is also easy for your competitors to do the same!

Social Media

Make the most of social media using social media channels such as Facebook, Twitter, Instagram, Snapchat and LinkedIn (e.g., create a Facebook page offering interesting content, discounts and offers).

Encourage existing customers and new ones to like your page, and use your page to show a gallery of past work. Regularly update the page and let everyone know.

Nearly two-thirds of American adults use social media now. This is a near tenfold increase within the last decade.

Each of the social media platforms is unique in its own right and requires unique ways of engagement. Try to identify which one fits with your customer profile.

Blogging

Regular blogs are a good low-cost way of keeping the business's presence in the public eye. You should try to create articles such as tip collections, industry best practice and top 10 lists.

If you can't create these yourself, this is an area where any expenditure will pay dividends, so a subcontractor who specializes in such things should be sought.

Press Releases

Make the most of your local or specialist press by sending regular releases to the relevant editor (you may need to research who this is). The releases could include details of the creation of extra jobs, a new business launch or a seminar you are organizing.

All these make for interesting news stories that the press are often desperate for.

This is a valuable exercise as it targets potential customers and it is free.

Advertising

Advertising needs to be focused not only in its message, but also on the audience receiving it. Web-hosting services allow businesses to do this with accuracy. Online advertising is paid on a 'per-click' basis, with the advertiser charged a fee (Facebook charges 80 cents) every time the advertisement is clicked on.

General advertisement is more for business awareness rather than selling specific products, and humor is becoming more important in this approach. The humor needs to be tailored to suit different markets.

Conventional advertisement mediums, such as TV, radio and newspaper advertisements, are very expensive and their effectiveness is difficult to monitor.

Online advertising can be cheaper, and can be made more targeted, such as Google Pay per Click.

Utilize websites such as Gumtree and Vivastreet where you can post advertisements for free.

Subcontract Web Content

You may accept that you are good at what you do, but have you got the imagination and flair to lift your content above that of your competitors?

There are many ways to share information – blogging, creating videos, hosting podcasts, designing infographics or producing authoritative articles.

You need to accept that you don't have the skills to create these things yourself and consider subcontracting to firms (like Upwork) that specialize in producing this work.

If the work you do is of a high enough standard, you may be considered an expert and included on others' websites.

If you have not got the resources to subcontract the work, you can reuse your own old content and update it.

Sponsorship and Publicity Stunts

Any story in the press regarding your business is free marketing, so any expense incurred to publicize the business is money well spent. Ways to do this can be as varied as

1. Creating a publicity stunt, for example the JT's Restaurant example in Chapter 3 could invite a celebrity to its opening night.

2. Do something for the community, for example, JT's again could host a charity lunch for the local Stroke Association.
3. Sponsor an event by providing services as a giveaway, for example, JT's again could offer a free meal for two as a prize.
4. Nominate the business for an award (if need be, even create the award – you won't be the first to do this!).

It is important if this approach is taken that the press is alerted in advance in order that they can be on hand to photograph the event for their publication.

The business can also seek opportunities to be interviewed as an industry expert on relevant matters, for example, JT's could provide a chef to comment on the latest diet fads.

Organize Contests or Free Gifts

The business should take advantage of the fact that everyone loves a free gift, by giving away items to build up brand awareness; for example, JT's could provide a free online recipe book to anyone who clicks onto their website.

Or they could give small gifts when presenting the bill at the end of the meal or offer a prize to anyone who completes a review of their experience.

Use Facebook groups to market test your product or services at a discount, offer free gifts and prizes (including the business logo) to encourage take-up.

Come up with a zany idea for a viral marketing campaign along the lines of the ice bucket challenge.

Joint Marketing

Consider working with other businesses in your location or industry on a joint marketing program. For example, JT's could team up with a local taxi business and each could benefit from the other's customer base.

The benefit of this approach is that the costs of any mailings etc. are shared.

Each could agree to distribute the other's business cards and flyers.

Other Marketing Methods

This first suggestion is something that irritates me, so be careful not to upset your customers by overusing this tactic. You could devise a telephone message that plays your promotions while customers are waiting to be connected to the correct advisor.

Mislead, but do not lie, in your marketing material, there is a fine art to this. It is very easy to get a different message across by omitting information, rather than including false information. This tactic should only be used on rare occasions, such as responding to an aggressive marketing campaign by one of your competitors.

You can exchange or buy customer lists and offer to pay the other business a commission for every sale you make. Just make sure that you have requested permission from your customers to share their details! You may receive commission from the other company's sales.

Use every opportunity to get your branding known, whether this is decals on office or retail windows, or the inclusion of the branding on the business's fleet of vehicles.

Details of any current sales promotions should be included on the letterheads of all letters and e-mails.

Your data capture system should include the facility to record customers' birth dates, and birthday coupons and surprise rewards could be sent to them as appropriate.

A key member of staff should be available and offer to speak at events, for example the chef at JT's could offer to speak at Women's Institute meetings, with the goal that the members may consider visiting the restaurant.

You could consider hosting a forum or website to provide assistance to potential customers.

Successful marketing is not only what brings the customers to your door, but it is also about influencing what they buy when they get there. A business's ability in this area can be key to its success.

Key to good marketing is not just to sell the product, but to sell the lifestyle it will bring. Motor manufacturers' advertising is often based on this model.

Marketing is all about influencing the buyers' behavior, and the use of new methods (called geo-target-marketing) can have a major impact on that buying behavior.

Geo-Marketing

Geo-marketing is the targeting of customers through the use of data collection and consumer profiling, so that a business can ensure that its products are on sale in the correct locations. One such example of this is impulse buying, either online or in actual locations.

Personalized pricing offers and tailored offers are possible through the collection of personal details, which is becoming increasingly popular. Some marketing strategies can involve the use of global positioning system (GPS) tracking.

Geo-marketing collects data of customers as they enquire and buy (mostly online, but occasionally by the customer completing in-store documentation).

To be successful, marketeers need to understand their customers' behavior, including what, why, where and how they buy.

Unknown to the customer, they go through a process before they purchase anything. This process is as follows:

1. Awareness of a need (often generated by advertising).
2. Research of the market to identify the products.

3. Evaluating alternatives available.
4. Purchase of the product and possibly an impulse buy.
5. Post-purchase evaluation/notification to contacts.

It is the marketeer's job to influence the customer's behavior during this process, and this can be done using numerous techniques. The process can vary from customer to customer, and may even vary for the same product if conditions change. With the use of data obtained through geo-marketing, it is easier to influence the customer's behavior.

Impulse Buying

Impulse buying is big business, and resources need to be applied to this area of a business's sales. Impulse buying is seen from the customer's perspective as an unplanned behavior. The marketeers know that this spontaneous, immediate and emotionally driven behavior can be easily influenced.

It has been estimated that up to 40% of all purchases are impulse purchases, and that figure is increasing as Internet providers are getting better at placing personalized advertising on web pages.

Estimates of impulse buys in supermarkets are as high as 60% of all purchases, and they are not just restricted to the chewing gum by the checkout. I have actually bought a car as an impulse buy.

Supermarkets are getting more sophisticated in using both in-store and promotional strategies to maximize impulse purchases, which are affected by a large number of things, including social and cultural influences, promotional activities and the environment of the store (or the user experience of the website).

There is one factor that stands above all others though: the perception of lower pricing. This is often enhanced by the vendor purporting to offer the product at a discount to its previous price, which has often proved not to be the case.

Push and Pull Marketing

The message in the advertising can be broken down further, and distinguished as to whether it forms part of a push and pull marketing strategy.

Push marketing is a form of advertising that sends a message to the customer. It can also be known as direct response marketing, and it targets a specific sector (such as baby-boomers) with messages and offers tailored to them. This is usually done by e-mail mail-shots or advertisements in periodicals.

Pull marketing is the opposite of push marketing, in that it pulls prospective customers to the business's website.

The age of the Internet has allowed customers access to a greater amount of information, and most undertake a significant amount of research before they decide upon a purchase (especially of expensive items). They read reviews, conduct keyword searches and ask online friends for suggestions.

Pull marketing can be used to provide those customers with answers to their questions, by providing details for them to discover and links to the business website. Businesses can do this by publishing their own blogs and reviews of their products.

Some businesses are less than honest in this process by providing their own fabricated customer reviews.

In terms of strategy, push marketing is about devising ways to display a product to your customers, usually by way of advertising that specific product. Direct mail-shots are often used to generate an interest in a specific product.

Pull marketing is more about creating customer awareness of your brand and services. Pull marketing is the process of making it easier for your customers to find you, both virtually and online. Pull marketing is more of an online method, used to ensure that customers are directed to a specific web page.

Discounts

Consumers are always responsive to bargains, and a discount offer to your customers immediately after their purchase can prove beneficial.

This offer can also be framed as a thank-you for the business, with a time-dependent special discount being offered for a further sale.

Always ask your customers how they found you, and why they have decided to use your services, so that you can monitor the effectiveness of your marketing efforts.

Networking

It is very important that a business lets the world know of its existence. A popular way of doing this is to network with other business owners and professional advisors. It is usual to join organizations such as

1. The local chamber of trade.
2. The Round Table.
3. A trade association; if there isn't one then start one up, you're sure to get an impressive job title as chairman or founder, which can be used to impress your customers.

Take up golf. A lot of business deals take place on a round of golf. You will gain 3 to 4 hours of uninterrupted access to your business target or business referrer.

You don't have to be particularly good at it, as people will enjoy beating you. You just need to be proficient enough to get around a golf course without holding up the groups playing behind you.

You can get away with hitting the occasional car in the car park. I can personally vouch for that.

Chapter 9

Now You've Got a Successful Business: What's the Next Step?

Once you've got the business set up and running smoothly, you can carry on as you are. But, given that you've been driven to achieve what you have, you're not likely to stop there. Your options, if you don't want to tread water, are

1. To open up extra outlets to expand the business or
2. To offer franchises to others to take on the business format or
3. To fine-tune the business to earn more

Extra Outlets

It would be stupid to think that a business's income could be doubled simply by opening a second outlet, but the move could provide an opportunity to enter a new market and provide a source of additional income, so it should not be discounted.

The process of opening additional outlets involves replicating a lot of the work to date, but the process is quicker and easier as many of the tasks of running the business have already been addressed.

In my experience, the main problems with running a business from multiple locations have been administrative, as the streamlining of costs, such as employees, can prove difficult.

Staff salaries should be the same at all locations, unless there are significant reasons which warrant a weighting. There may need to be a requirement to pay higher salaries to attract staff to a less than salubrious area.

Management of the business can prove a problem unless one of the proprietors is present at the new location, as the monitoring of staff remotely can be difficult.

But, setting up another outlet can provide the chance to offer staff new management roles and the opportunity to extend themselves.

Some businesses have been known to set up similar businesses under a pseudo-name, providing the same goods, in order not to be seen to be monopolizing the market.

Consumers can often be fooled by this tactic and switch brand loyalty to the new 'competitor'.

Franchising

An option that is available to a business that cannot be bothered investing time and effort in expanding its activities is that of franchising its business activities to a third party.

The 'purchase' of a franchise has already been discussed in Chapter 4, and the 'sale' of a franchise will involve the reverse of the matters already covered.

Fine-Tuning the Business

The business should be continually monitoring its activities and looking at all avenues to increase its profits.

The following exercise will show you that, with little changes, you can double the profits that your business makes. But first you need to know the basics of how a business makes a profit.

A business generates income (turnover) by selling products or services to customers. A profitable business is one where the costs are less than the income.

The following is a summary of a basic business's results.

	£
Income	8000
Expenses	2000
Profit	6000

This business has 40 customers who spend £100 twice a year, hence the income of £8000.

With a few tweaks the profit could be more than doubled:

1. The customer numbers could be increased by 7.5% to 43.
2. The spend per visit increased by 6% to £106.
3. The visits increased from two to three per year.
4. Costs could be reduced by 25% from £2000 to £1500, by concentrating on the business expenditure.

Overall, there could be a significant increase in the business profitability to £12,174 (the following is a revised account).

	£
Income	12,674
Expenses	1,500
Profit	12,174

Cost Cutting

A business can cut costs by looking at industry averages, and comparing the business expenditure with that of the competition in order to reduce any excesses.

The main costs are usually staff costs, which are the hardest cost to cut. A review of this expenditure will often disclose areas of pay inequality and wastage, and can produce significant savings for the business.

Often, the business owner has an illogical attachment to the staff, or a fear of industrial action by disgruntled employees if a pay cut or freeze was to be imposed, and may find it difficult to cut the level of pay.

Businesses need to audit all expenses and look for opportunities to make savings. It is very easy to build a culture/system where money is being unnecessarily wasted.

'Repairing rather than replacing' seems to have lost its relevance in our throwaway society.

It is common for businesses to subcontract labor for far more of the cost of employing them, but this is deceiving, as discussed in Chapter 5, as the employment of staff brings with it long-term liabilities in terms of staff benefits.

A cost savings review may involve these policies being revisited.

Cheaper alternative suppliers should be reviewed on an ongoing basis.

If, as a result of your cost-cutting exercise, you decide to transfer your business to a cheaper supplier, I would advise that you explore how they are able to undercut your existing suppliers. If their cut prices come as a result of child labor in third-world countries, you need to be aware that their business ethics may be associated with your own, should they ever be investigated.

A business needs to review expense headings regularly and explore every opportunity to cost cut. There is a lot to be said for the old saying 'look after the pennies, and the pounds look after themselves', as the mindset that creates can prevent expenditure getting out of hand.

In recent years, motor manufacturers have dispensed with providing spare wheels on new cars, opting instead to provide a puncture repair kit in order to reduce costs. If the savings of doing this were £50 per vehicle, the cost savings do not look significant.

But on sales of 300,000 cars a year, the total savings are £15 million a year, and given that a model can last for more than 10 years or more, the total savings could be £150 million.

But, if like me, you have been through the trauma of having to use one of these kits, you will agree that they are not fit for purpose. I would not buy another car with one of these kits again, and the loss of my business and others like me will soon eat into the £150 million savings.

There have been more successful attempts at cost cutting by businesses, which on the face of it look trivial, but when scaled up have accounted for significant profit increases.

As shown in the preceding example, if the business can successfully reduce its cost, and marginally increase its income, the profitability increase can be significant.

Reviewing Sales Promotions and Marketing Campaigns

We should now look again at some of the tried and tested methods of marginally increasing a business's income, using some of the marketing techniques discussed in Chapter 8.

1. BOGOF – buy one get one free. Not only a good way of moving stock, it also encourages customers to buy more than they intended to. But it does reduce profitability.
2. Money off/free offer vouchers, after a minimum spend. A local business I frequent, often uses this ploy, by

offering a free goods voucher after a minimum spend of £5. It is doubly successful for the business in that I am often tempted to make an extra visit to their business upon receipt of the voucher, and I also usually spend in excess of £20 on my visit.

3. Impulse buys situated next to the tills. Studies have shown that up to 40% of expenditure by consumers is through impulse buys. The main impulse buy items are often situated at key spots throughout the store/website that ensure the customer will notice them.

4. Rewards for recommending new customers. Existing customers are directed to think that they are part of an exclusive group and can improve their friends' well-being by recommending them to take up an offer. In return, they are offered a discount on their own future purchases.

5. Collection of customers' details by stealth or buying from a third party. It is difficult for anyone to buy anything in-store or online without registering their details as a customer, and unless they are able to avoid it, unwittingly agree to receive future correspondence from the vendor regarding offers, etc.

Many retailers offer loyalty cards to customers, and in the process of applying for them customers, again, unwittingly agree to receive further details from the vendor.

While mentioning loyalty, it may be an appropriate time to discuss the offers given to new customers versus those offered to existing customers. Insurance companies appear to have a marketing strategy that focuses more on the acquisition of new customers, in that they are offered better deals than the business's existing customers.

This has led to a lot of customer dissatisfaction, and a reduction in brand loyalty, with the sector working far harder to satisfy the same number of customers.

This has been exacerbated by the large number of comparison websites, and until the insurers take back control of their sector and act as a whole to refuse to provide online quotes, the situation may get worse.

It is also possible to buy customer details that have been acquired by other businesses, and produce a tailored list of prospects from the information provided; however, this comes with a cost, which if you are unwilling to incur, your competitors will pay.

Many businesses gain the information they need online by utilizing cookies. These are files that are downloaded onto your Internet-connected device when you visit a website for the first time.

The next time you visit the site, the cookie notifies the website that you have been there before, and the site then personalizes the pages you will see.

Cookies can also record how long you spend on each page and the links you clicked, and can analyze your search to identify your preferences in terms of page layouts and colors.

In recent years, the banking and utility sectors have been very active in marginally increasing their income, often with their customers not realizing that they have been put on a higher tariff or are paying a higher fee for their services. This has often been done by stealth, and intentionally so.

This has shown how much contempt they have for their customers, who often refuse to leave to try a competitor. Their brand loyalty has suffered, but their customers still remain:

1. Out of comfort
2. Out of resignation
3. For fear of the unknown/of changing

These disgruntled customers are often quick to leave once the regulatory authorities introduce measures to make 'switching' easier.

For this reason, I would not advise that you treat your customers with the same contempt as these larger businesses do, as satisfied customers should be the cornerstone of your business and are essential for a successful long-term business model.

Why then, do these larger businesses adopt these dubious business practices? The answer is that they concentrate on short-term profitability (for maximum dividends to shareholders) without considering the long-term costs (which often will not affect those responsible for incurring them).

The recent financial scandals involving the mis-selling of financial products have resulted in those businesses being subject to substantial fines while those responsible are long retired receiving substantial pensions.

This brings us again onto the topic of business morality, which is maybe a subject for a separate book?

Chapter 10

How It Can Go Horribly Wrong

If you find yourself in the position that you are unable to clear your liabilities as they fall due, you are insolvent and need to cease trading with immediate effect.

Insolvency can occur unexpectedly, but often it comes after months, if not years, of desperately trying to keep the business afloat.

Major Reasons for Insolvencies

The reasons for insolvency are many, and I include the more likely as follows:

1. *Dominant customer*: Often, a business's downfall can be as a result of it successfully gaining a contract with a major customer. In these circumstances, if the customer is of a much larger size than the business and thus can control the relationship, this can often lead to sales being made for less than cost.

An example of this is where a low-cost airline (a large business) signs up to use a small regional airport as part of its operations.

The contract will usually stipulate that the airport provides the services that are usually found at major hub airports, such as catering facilities and tax-free shopping.

The small airport then incurs significant costs in beefing up its infrastructure, which reduces the profitability of the contract which it has just acquired and, more importantly, means that it is unable to trade at a profit should it lose that contract.

By acquiring the contract, the small airport will be able to increase its income, but it has become reliant upon another business for its future prosperity.

What often compounds this situation is that the small airport will have lost all their other customers in their attempt to please their new main customer.

Supermarkets are adept at using these arrangements with their small suppliers, knowing that they could ruin them if they pulled their contracts. This is how they can command keen prices.

Businesses which acquire major customers need to ensure that their contract does not leave their business exposed in any way should the customer attempt to renegotiate the terms.

A contract gained with a large customer can often become a poisoned chalice!

2. *Illness*: If the proprietor becomes unexpectedly ill with a life-threatening or serious disease, the business can suffer due to their absence.

It is probable that no one else in the business will have the drive to continue working at the pace of the proprietor.

As a result, the business's activities will stall and more likely cease, leading to a cessation of the business.

The borrowings of the business will, therefore, no longer be funded, and cash flow will become an issue.

To compound the issue, the proprietor will find, due to lack of income, that his personal liabilities will increase, and he will demand more income from the business.

This is a cocktail for business and/or personal bankruptcy, and unless there is adequate insurance cover in place, this is the end of the line for the business and its employees.

It is interesting to note that 78% of bankruptcies in the USA are as a result of an illness.

I would strongly advise that every business protects itself against this scenario.

3. *Bad credit control*: Most entrepreneurs are sales driven and tend to build up good relationships with their customers, many of whom become personal friends.

As a result of this, the proprietor tends to be lax when those customers exceed their credit terms, and the proprietor often overrules their employed credit controllers who are advising them to aggressively chase the debt.

This isn't a problem when the debt is fairly insignificant, but I have personally been involved in two insolvencies when the 'friend's' debt has caused the business to fail.

The 'everyone's in the same boat' discussions in the golf club bar can blind the entrepreneur as to the real financial position of his own and his customer's business.

Often, one business will drag down the other.

4. *Using the tax man as a source of capital*: Given the way the self-assessment system operates, it is easy for a business to under-declare their true liabilities and pay less than they should do.

It is more convenient to put aside a VAT bill if one of your other creditors is being very insistent on immediate payment, especially if HM Customs & Excise are not expecting the payment.

The problem is that once a payment has been under-declared successfully, and other creditors are demanding their dues, it is easy to do it again.

This is not a wise thing to do as once the authorities realize what has happened, they will demand immediate payment of the true amount due plus interest and penalties.

As this could happen at any time, it leaves the business in a precarious position, as a large amount for immediate payment may fall due at any time.

If HM Customs & Excise are not paid immediately, they become aware of the underpayment, have the right to visit the business premises and seize property to the value of the liability.

Other Reasons for Failure

Other than the foregoing reasons, most business failures are caused by a lack of

1. *Business model/budget/plan*: Businesses that operate without a financial budget are taking a huge gamble, as a business that is unaware that cash flows are negative can't take action to correct the position.
2. *Resources (people/time/money)*: Often, businesses promise to supply products within time frames they can't achieve, and because of a lack of resources (biting off more than they can chew) they fail to deliver. The result is a disgruntled customer looking elsewhere for their needs.
3. *Marketing strategy*: It's no good having the best products in the world if no one knows about them. Getting customers to the door is key to financial success.
4. *Experience in the market*: Many insolvencies have been caused by businesses entering into markets in which they have no experience. This could be either inexperience in commercial operations or lack of knowledge of business practices.

Examples of this are shown in the Examples of Disasters section later in this chapter.

5. *Dishonesty*: Either within the business or of those the business deals with. Sometimes, the dishonesty of the other business can be quite legal, and covered within contracts signed in ignorance.

   The most famous case of dishonesty bringing down a business is that of Nick Leeson and Barings Bank. Nick Leeson incurred losses of $1.4 billion in February 1995, while dishonestly trying to cover up bad trades that he had made.

   Nick Leeson was given a six-and-a-half-year prison sentence for his actions.

   Although I have attributed the fall of Barings Bank to dishonesty, it was, in fact, due to their bad management, allowing him to hide the losses he made over four years from the company's auditors.

6. *Contractual liabilities*: Businesses can find themselves contracted to customers or suppliers on terms that are disadvantageous for the business.

7. *Aggressive competitors*: Many businesses have failed after a price war with a business rival. Often, the relationships become so embittered that logic is thrown out of the window, and the business takes decisions that can cost the business and the jobs of all those who work in it.

8. *Greedy, immoral bankers*: I have had experience of and know of a lawyer making a living from prosecuting those responsible for the misdeeds of the banking profession. Businesses in financial difficulties have been saddled with unaffordable restructuring costs purely to earn the 'adviser' commission on sales of inappropriate products.

Insolvency and Liquidators

Often, when a business owner feels that he has come to the end of the line because he is unable to clear all his debts, he will call in an insolvency specialist, who will review the state of play to see if there is anything left to salvage.

With the agreement of the creditors, the insolvency practitioner can put together a plan that may involve the business only partly clearing its debts. This can be either an individual or a company voluntary arrangement (CVA), depending upon whether the business is incorporated or not.

Voluntary Arrangements

Individual/company voluntary arrangements are essentially a deal between the insolvent individual/company (the debtor) and their creditors, which effectively places a legal ring-fence around the debtor and stops creditors attacking them.

The voluntary arrangement is an agreement with the creditors where the debtor agrees to pay all or part of their debts.

The debtor agrees to make regular payments to the insolvency practitioner, who divides this up to repay the creditors.

Once the insolvency practitioner has been appointed, usually within a month, they will prepare a report on the financial position of the debtor. Based on this report, they will construct a plan summarizing what they consider the debtor can afford to repay.

They will forward this plan to all the creditors, and the voluntary arrangement will start if the creditors holding 75% of the debts agree to it. It will apply to all the creditors, even those who disagree to it.

A voluntary arrangement stops any creditor taking action for their debts and allows a viable but struggling debtor to repay some, or all, of their debts over a period time to be agreed.

An example of a voluntary arrangement follows.

Draft Example of a Company Voluntary Arrangement (CVA) Proposal

Insolvency Act
  Proposal for a company voluntary arrangement (CVA)

Name of Company:	Lostit Limited
Business Address:	Skid Row
	Birmington
	England
Name of Nominee:	Pick, them, bones
	Licensed Insolvency Practitioners
	Where it's at
	Birmington
Date of Proposal:	.... 20 ....

(Note that all references to 'Rule' numbers in the following are to the insolvency rules.)

Introduction (Rule 1.3(1))

Lostit Limited was formed in 1999.

The principal areas of business are the production and sale of quality electric guitars.

The directors are Mr. LesPaul and Mr. Stratocaster.

The first two years of trading (1999–2001) produced losses and the company then moved into profit in its third year.

2003 saw the loss of a major, high earning account worth some £150,000 per annum. Around the same time there was a general downturn in work levels as the music industry turned its back on quality blues guitar music. This made staff cut-backs necessary.

As the audit for 2004 progressed, a growing number of discrepancies in the internal accounting procedures became apparent, which meant that the previous year's results had to be restated, turning what had been a profit into a loss.

Swift action was needed to avert the collapse of the company. Mr. LesPaul took control of finances and installed finance software to prepare regular management accounts. Further staff cuts were made. All salaries were reduced with the directors taking the largest share and pension payments were ceased. Mr. LesPaul and Mr. Stratocaster sold their company cars and, in addition, injected personal monies. The structure of the company was reviewed and new budgets and working disciplines introduced. Unprofitable work was shed and, on the advice of the auditors, the directors met with an insolvency practitioner to discuss the situation and further remedial actions were then put in place. That insolvency practitioner considered that it was possible for the company to trade out of the difficulties.

In mid-2005, the bank account was moved from StitchMup Bank to SqueezeMdry Bank. In addition to an overdraft facility of £200,000, Mr. LesPaul and Mr. Stratocaster took out a further personal loan of £40,000, which was injected into the company. The company overdraft was secured by personal guarantees and backed up by outside security. The company earned a modest profit for the year to 31 March 2006. As a consequence, the pressures from creditors eased considerably.

It had been the intention for Mr. LesPaul to withdraw from the business at the end of 2007. However, with the change of emphasis in the nature of the business, Mr. LesPaul proposed that he should bring this forward and presented Mr. Stratocaster with a proposal for an earlier withdrawal. In this, Mr. LesPaul proposes to make a loan to the company of £115,000 and also pay off half of the outstanding balance on the £40,000 personal loan that he and Mr. Stratocaster had taken with SqueezeMdry Bank. This withdrawal would also benefit the company by way of reducing overheads. In exchange for this capital injection, it is proposed that Mr. LesPaul will take a second debenture behind SqueezeMdry Bank.

September had seen the end of a large ongoing contract. This coincided with a number of bad debts, including a major client that was experiencing its own financial difficulties, which resulted in wrangling for payment and prompting the company to instigate legal proceedings. As a result, only a percentage of the outstanding debt has been received and over a period of months this has had an extremely negative effect on the company's cash flow.

October and November 2006 figures were disappointing. In the meantime, the company had gained a considerable amount of new and profitable business. However, the directors could see that cash flow benefits would not arise from the increased work for at least 8 weeks.

The future of Lostit Limited shows a substantial change of direction with the planned resignation of Mr. LesPaul. The traditional core element of the business – the work pioneered by Mr. Stratocaster – will remain.

A new division of the business under the control of a senior employee, Mr. Telecaster, is generating increased business with a high element of profit and low purchases and this is intended to be the main area of business development in the future.

The new division has continued to attract new clients in recent months, and there is very little competition for the new lines of guitars.

The new products are being launched on 1 April and we have clients on board and the general response is very encouraging.

Confirmed contracts for the new line-up total £244,000 and there is also the prospect of winning additional specific contracts of £171,000.

The directors considered placing the company into creditors voluntary liquidation and then restarting a new company. They concluded, however, that as the prospects for the business now appeared to be promising, they would wish to put forward a CVA. The objective being to repay all creditors in full.

The directors discussed the position with the company bankers and on their advice sought guidance from the auditors. The auditors advised the directors to meet with insolvency practitioners. The directors met with the insolvency advisors for the first time on the 14 December 2006. Since that time, information has been amassed to prepare this proposal for all creditors.

It is apparent from the statement of affairs shown at Schedule 1 that if the company were now placed into creditors voluntary liquidation, neither preferential nor unsecured creditors would receive any dividend at all as the work in progress would then become worthless.

On a liquidation, it can be seen from that same statement that SqueezeMdry Bank would suffer a shortfall of some £138,000.

Lostit Limited is essentially a 'people business' and it is in the light of a substantial order book that the following proposals are made.

Proposals (Rule 1.3(2))

2.1 It is proposed that:

2.1.1 The company pay into this voluntary arrangement, the sum of £3500 per month for a 4 year period.

2.1.2 Mr. LesPaul introduce £115,000 into the business, which will be used to reduce the SqueezeMdry Bank overdraft. Mr. LesPaul would then be granted a second debenture.

It is further proposed that Mr. LesPaul would be treated as a 'deferred creditor' and would not share in any part of the dividends paid to creditors out of the pool of money arising from the £3500 per month payable into this arrangement.

2.1.3. The 'associated' creditors totaling £94,745 also be treated as deferred creditors.

Additionally, it is proposed that Mr. Gretch (Mr. Stratocaster's father-in-law) capitalize his outstanding loan totaling £79,745, which is included in the total of £94,745.

2.1.4 In relation to SqueezeMdry Bank (The Bank) the following proposals are made:

- That the company collect in the existing debtors totaling £64,000 and pay that in its entirety to the bank. (The bank is entitled to those monies in any event as they hold a fixed charge over trade debtors.)
- That the old bank account be frozen at its present balance of £198,000 and that the £64,000 expected to be received in from the existing debtors be paid into that old account.
- That the £115,000 to be paid in by Mr. LesPaul be paid into that 'old' bank account.

The consequences of the foregoing transactions are

- That the directors expect the old bank account to reduce as follows:

	£	£
Present bank balance		198,000
Less:		
Expected debtor proceeds	60,000	
Cash from Mr. LesPaul	115,000	
		175,000
Revised bank balance		23,000

■ That the bank considers providing the company with a 'new' overdraft facility based on the cash flow and profit projections shown at Schedules 8 and 9.

(The directors would continue to provide outside security to SqueezeMdry Bank for the residual balance on the 'old' account and the balance on the new account.)

■ That the company pay to the bank a monthly sum of £1000 (being capital and interest) to extinguish the residual balance on the 'old' account over a period.

2.1.5 The effect of these proposals in terms of the dividend payable to preferential and unsecured creditors is calculated at Schedule 6 attached.

From that schedule, it should be noted that

■ Preferential creditors would be paid in full on the first anniversary of the arrangement.

■ Unsecured creditors would receive dividends on the second, third and fourth anniversaries. It is proposed that each of these dividends be one-third of the amount owed to creditors, such that all unsecured creditors will have been repaid in full by the time of the fourth anniversary.

2.2 To minimize Supervisor's costs, it is additionally proposed that the Supervisor will not be involved with the subsequent trading of this company, if this proposal is agreed except to the extent set out in Clause 2.19.

2.3 Schedule 1 to this proposal lists all of the assets of the company showing estimated net realizable values, on a going concern basis, less amounts owing to secured preferential and unsecured creditors.

2.4 It is proposed to deal with the claims of creditors as follows:

Secured Creditors

SqueezeMdry Bank is the only secured creditor. SqueezeMdry Bank has a fixed and floating charge over the assets of the company.

Nothing in this proposal, however, restricts the rights of SqueezeMdry Bank at present or in the future of appointing either a book debt receiver or administrative receiver.

A 'new' bank account has already been set up with SqueezeMdry Bank for post-CVA trading. An overdraft on that new account will be requested by the directors based on the attached cash flow forecasts (see Schedule 9). The balance on the 'new' account is presently a positive figure of £11,769.

Preferential Creditors

It is proposed to deal with the claims of preferential creditors as follows:

- Preferential creditors arising from the pre-CVA period will enjoy the same priority, as if there had been a creditors voluntary liquidation on the day set for the meeting of creditors to consider this CVA.
- It is further proposed that a new additional class of preferential creditor would arise should there be any failure of this arrangement. Such creditors would be calculated within the meaning of Sections 175 and 386 of the Insolvency Act 1986 with the 'relevant date' being the date on which the Supervisor issues a 'Certificate of Failure of the arrangement'.
- Pre-CVA and post-CVA preferential creditors are to enjoy the same priority, one as against the other, in relation to all of the unpledged assets.

Deferred Creditors

The following creditors are classed as 'deferred':

	£
Proposed – Mr. LesPaul – Loan	115,000
Existing loans from the shareholders and directors	94,745
Total deferred creditors	209,745

It is proposed that deferred creditors receive no dividend over the 4-year life of the arrangement.

It is proposed that £79,745 of the existing loans be capitalized.

Once all pre-CVA preferential and unsecured creditors have been paid in full, the two classes of creditors shown previously will no longer be classified as deferred.

Unsecured Creditors

Pre-CVA unsecured creditors will rank pari passu for payment. Any such claims that had been inadvertently omitted from the attached statement of affairs or the arrangement and whose total debts do not exceed 10% of the total of all claims lodged will be invited to claim in and be bound by the arrangement. This is subject, however, to the proviso that any dividend already paid will not be disturbed, but lost dividends can be made up from any future distributions.

In the event of this CVA failing, then post-CVA unsecured creditors will have a claim as ordinary unsecured creditors then ranking equally with pre-CVA unsecured creditors.

Associated Creditors

Those creditors 'associated' with or 'connected' with the company within the meaning of Section 249 of the 1986 Insolvency Act are set out in detail at Schedule 5 attached.

All 'associated' creditors are proposed to be treated as 'deferred'.

2.5 To the directors' knowledge, there are no circumstances giving rise to the possibility, in the event that the company should go into liquidation, of claims under:

■ Section 238 (transactions at an undervalue)
■ Section 239 (preferences except to the extent referred to in Paragraph 4.3)
■ Section 244 (extortionate credit transactions)
■ Section 245 (invalid floating charges)

However, there are 66 creditors – each being for a sum less than £200, which together total £3637. Those creditors have not been included in this document as it is proposed that the company immediately settle those creditors in full. The directors of the company are of the opinion that that would be the most cost-effective way of dealing with such small creditors.

2.6 No liabilities of the company have been guaranteed by any other party except that the liability to SqueezeMdry Bank has been guaranteed by Mr. LesPaul and Mr. Stratocaster.

2.7 It is proposed that the CVA last 4 years.

2.8 Distributions to creditors and amounts thereof are proposed to be made as follows:

Estimated Date	Amount Payable	Type of Payment/To Whom Payable	Estimated Pence in the Pound
	£		
Mar 2008	21,966	Preferential	100p
Mar 2009	40,322	Unsecured	33.3p
Mar 2010	40,321	Unsecured	33.3p
Mar 2011	40,321	Unsecured	33.4p
Totals	120,964		100p

2.9 A reconciliation is shown at Schedule 6 detailing the total amount to be realized into the arrangement less the costs of the arrangement, to provide the net figures being the amount distributable shown above.

Any creditor who has not lodged his claim having received 21 days' notice will be excluded from that dividend, but if the claim is lodged late, that creditor will be entitled to make up that amount from future realizations.

2.10 Nominee's fees for producing the CVA proposal and for dealing with all matters up to and including the date of the creditors meeting is proposed to be in the sum of £3500 plus VAT.

It is further proposed that the Nominee recover all third-party disbursements and also be entitled to any costs and disbursements including legal costs that he incurs in connection with any appeal following from the meeting of creditors, unless the court orders otherwise.

2.11 It is proposed that Supervisor's fees be based on the time costs of the Supervisor's firm.

It is also proposed that the Supervisor's remuneration shall be calculated by reference to the time spent by the Supervisor and his staff.

The Supervisor's fees and expenses shall rank ahead of the claims of creditors and after any costs payable to the Nominee.

The Supervisor will be entitled to be reimbursed his costs above any other expenses incurred in bringing or defending any action in the arrangement, unless the court orders otherwise.

2.12 The directors of the company do not propose to offer any additional personal guarantees to creditors in relation to this proposed CVA proposal.

2.13 The Supervisor shall open a current account at the Fatcats Bank and all payments to the Supervisor shall be promptly paid into such account. The Supervisor shall have discretion to invest funds surplus to the immediate requirements of the arrangement on deposit on the money market from time to time, pending any distribution of such funds.

2.14 If upon termination of the arrangement, any funds held for the purposes of payment to creditors remain in the hands of the Supervisor because any creditor (a) has failed to claim at all or (b) has not cashed any check forwarded to him or (c) can no longer be traced or, if after the voluntary arrangement has been concluded, the then former Supervisor receives funds that were not anticipated to have been receivable at the time of closure, such funds will be dealt with as follows:

If the aggregate of such funds after costs exceeds £1000, a further distribution shall be made to those creditors who are able to participate therein, less the (former) Supervisor's outstanding time costs and disbursements, if any. If such funds, however, amount to less than that amount, the costs of a distribution are not justified and accordingly, the balance will be returned to the company after deducting any amounts outstanding for any outstanding time costs and disbursement of the (former) Supervisor.

2.15 During the course of the voluntary arrangement, the new trading of the company will not be carried out under the auspices of the Nominee or Supervisor or in the name of either of them and the Nominee and Supervisor will not be involved in or in any way responsible for such new trading.

2.16 During the continuation of this CVA, any new credit taken by the company during the course of the arrangement is to be settled by the company from the proposed new SqueezeMdry Bank CVA account. That new bank account being operated by the directors of the company and not by the Supervisor. In the event of the failure of this arrangement, any positive balance on that account will be treated as being available to meet the costs of the arrangement and of the Nominee and Supervisor and secondly to be available by way of setoff against the 'old' SqueezeMdry Bank account.

2.17 The Supervisor's functions shall be

1. To receive all funds payable into the arrangement (i.e. £3500 monthly).

2. To prove all creditors' claims.
3. To make distributions to creditors in due order of priority and on the due dates shown in Paragraph 2.1.
4. To retain solicitors, agents or other professional advisors if required for the beneficial purposes of the arrangement at the expense of the estate.
5. To receive monthly profit and loss accounts and balance sheets. To forward all creditors annually a summary of the company results and as to the general progress of the arrangement.
6. To authorize the release of funds from the estate to defend disputed claims where appropriate.
7. To review on a regular basis whether the CVA has failed in accordance with the criteria set out in Paragraph 2.19.

2.18 It is proposed that the Supervisor of the arrangement shall be Big Bob, the biscuit eater, who is qualified to act as an insolvency practitioner in relation to the company.

2.19 These clauses deal with the control of the CVA and the Supervisor's duty should the arrangement be declared a failure.

2.19.1 The arrangement shall be declared a failure if:

1. The first instalment of £3500 is not received within 7 days of the arrangement being approved at the creditors' meeting called to consider this proposal.
2. Two consecutive payments of the monthly instalments are not received on the due dates. The due date of each instalment, except the first, being on the 31st of each month.
3. Monthly payments of interest are not paid to SqueezeMdry Bank
4. Monthly profit and loss accounts and balance sheets with supporting schedules of all key figures are not provided to the Supervisor within 30 days after the end of each monthly accounting period.

2.19.2 If any of the four instances referred to in Paragraph 2.19.1 arise the Supervisor will immediately:

- Circularize all creditors and issue a 'Certificate of Failure' of the arrangement.
- Apply to the court for the company to be compulsory wound up should the directors not sign notices to call a creditors' meeting under Section 98 of the 1986 Insolvency Act within 7 days of the issue of the Certificate of Failure.

Alterations to the Proposal (Rule 1.3(3))

This director's proposal for a CVA may be amended with the agreement of the creditors at the forthcoming creditors' meeting.

Realization of Assets

4.1 It is proposed that the sums realized from the debtors now existing be collected in and paid to SqueezeMdry Bank under the terms of their debenture.

4.2 It is proposed that the work in progress at the date of the creditors' meeting be utilized as working capital in the CVA period.

4.3 It is proposed that the vehicles on finance not be sold but instead used in the continuing business.

4.4 It is proposed that the monthly sum of £3500 be paid to the Supervisor on the due dates by standing order.

We, the directors and shareholders of the company, confirm that this document fairly sets out our proposals to the creditors for a company voluntary arrangement and that to the best of our knowledge and belief all statements herein are true.

Dated this .... day of .... 20 ....

Signed ...., ...

      Director   **Director**

(The directors should sign each page and schedules of the proposal)

I received the written notice on the .... day of ...., 20.........

Big Bob

I consent to act as Nominee and Supervisor

Big Bob

Index to Appendices

1. Statement of affairs at ...., 20...........
2. Notes to statement of affairs.
3. Notes re assets subject to Hire Purchase and Lease Purchase Agreements.
4. Schedule of Unsecured Creditors.
5. Schedule of 'Associated' Creditors.
6. Calculations of Dividend.
7. Statutory Information.
8. Profit Forecast
9. Cash Flow Forecast
10. Tabulation of Past Results

Schedule 1

Lostit Limited Statement of Affairs as at............. 20.........

	£	£
Assets specifically pledged		
Trade debtors	64,119	
Less: Provision for bad debts	4,119	
		60,000
Less: SqueezeMdry Bank – 'Old' Account		(198,472)
Shortfall to floating charge		(138,472)
Assets on hire purchase		
See Schedule		3,326
Assets not specifically pledged		
Work in progress		32,391
SqueezeMdry Bank – 'New' Account		11,769
		(90,986)
Less preferential creditors		
HM Customs & Excise – VAT	7,243	
Inland Revenue – PAYE	14,723	
Employees	Nil	
		(21,966)
Deficiency as regards floating charge holder		(112,952)
Less unsecured creditors		
Per Schedule 4	120,964	
Associated creditors per Schedule 5	94,745	
		(215,709)
Deficiency as regards unsecured creditors		(328,661)
Less share capital		120,000
Overall deficiency		(448,661)

Schedule 2

Lostit Limited – notes to statement of affairs

1. At the time of preparing this statement of affairs, the motor vehicles on hire purchase arrangements have not been professionally valued.
2. The fixtures, fittings and equipment used in the business are held mainly under the terms of lease agreements.
   The remaining such assets not under lease arrangements are considered by the directors to be of minimal value.
3. No provision has been made in the statement of affairs for costs that would arise in respect of employees (such as redundancy) if the company were to be placed in liquidation.
4. Should there be a liquidation, the work in progress shown in the statement would be of no value.

Schedule 3

Lostit Limited – assets subject to hire purchase or lease purchase arrangements

		£	£
1.	Registered car		
	(acquired 06.07.04)		
	at estimated valuation	5000	
	Less: owing to finance company	4168	
	EQUITY		832
2.	Registered car		
	at estimated valuation	5000	
	Less: owing to finance company	2506	
			2494
	Per statement of affairs		3326

Schedule 4

Lostit Limited – schedule of unsecured creditors

Here, there would be a listing of all of the creditors to show
their names and the amount owing to each creditor. Likewise,
there would be detailed lists of associated creditors in a separate schedule (Schedule 5).

Schedule 6

**Lostit Limited – calculation of dividend returns to pref-
erential and unsecured creditors**

   Notes

   1. It is proposed that the monies loaned to the company, to
      date, by the directors and shareholders totaling £94,745
      are not repaid until all secured, preferential and unse-
      cured creditors are repaid in full (i.e., the associated credi-
      tors will be classed as 'deferred creditors'). In any event, it
      is proposed that £79,745 of that figure be capitalized.
   2. SqueezeMdry Bank will be treated as an unsecured credi-
      tor to the extent that their loan is not covered by trade
      debtors. For the purpose of the calculation that follows,
      that figure is estimated at £138,000. The calculation of

that figure is shown on Schedule 1. It is proposed that the £115,000 injection by .... be used to reduce the bank borrowing.

After collecting currently outstanding debts, the liability to SqueezeMdry Bank would be £23,000 approximately. It is proposed that SqueezeMdry Bank receive a £1000 per month repayment of capital and interest during the life of this arrangement. SqueezeMdry Bank would not share in the accumulated pool created from the Supervisor's realizations of £3500 per month.

3. The proposed injection by .... of £115,000 on a second debenture be treated as a deferred creditor.

4. The creditors then ranking for dividend and the priority between them is estimated as follows:

		£
4.1	Preferential Creditors	21,966
4.2	Unsecured Creditors	120,964

		£	£
5.	Amount receivable into the arrangement		
	48 months at £3,500 per month		168,000
	Less: Costs of the arrangement		
	Nominee's fees	3,500	
	Supervisor's fees	12,000	
	Insurance bond	1,000	
	Disbursements	1,500	
	Provision for any other costs	7,000	
			25,000

Distributable to creditors		143,000
Distributed as follows:		
Preferential Creditors		21,966
(Dividend payable on the first anniversary of the arrangement)		
Unsecured Creditors		120,964
(Dividends payable annually on each anniversary of the arrangement until all such creditors are repaid in full)		
Total Distribution		<u>142,930</u>

Schedule 7

Lostit Limited – statutory information

Details regarding the company, its directors and shareholders etc. would usually be included here.

6. Audited accounts

The last audited accounts filed with the Registrar of Companies were those for the year ended 31 March 2006.

Those accounts were prepared on a going concern basis. The auditor's report notes the following:

'Fundamental uncertainty'... 'During June 2006, the company directors were able to renegotiate banking facilities for the company which is dependent upon the company's achievement of the projections prepared by the directors for the period ended 31 March, 2007'.

'The company directors have also had to continue to make arrangements with company creditors to discuss settlement periods for outstanding liabilities. The directors consider that provided the creditors continue to support the company by allowing a further period for settlement, then the company will be able to continue to trade for the foreseeable future'.

The auditor's report was therefore qualified for these fundamental uncertainties.

The net deficiency shown on the balance sheet at 31 March 2006 was £296,815.

Register of Charges

5.1 On 01.12.2001, SqueezeMdry Bank registered a fixed and floating charge over all of the assets of the company.

5.2 It is understood that the bank has additional security on assets personally owned by certain directors of the company.

The directors have compiled a detailed profit forecast to back up the summary figures shown above.

As you can see from the previous example, the benefits of a company voluntary arrangement are

1. The directors stay in control of the company.
2. It can stop legal actions like winding up petitions.
3. It allows the opportunity for the business to be sold or refinanced.
4. It can quickly improve cash flow.
5. It can stop pressure from tax, VAT and PAYE while the company voluntary arrangement is being prepared.
6. It can rapidly cut costs.
7. It can terminate employment, leases, onerous supply contracts and all with nil cash cost.
8. You can terminate directors' and/or managers' contracts as well.
9. You can terminate onerous customer/supplier' contracts.

10. It's a good deal for creditors as they retain a customer and receive some of their debt back over time, usually between 20p and 100p in every £1 of debts.
11. It can give you more control of your assets than a bankruptcy.

The process has been part of UK law since 1986 and is one of the government's preferred rescue options.

The Process of Insolvency

Insolvency, when it happens, is actually caused by loss of capital, loss of revenue and loss of credit. A business in the process of becoming insolvent really is like 'death by inches'. Although many businesses are all too well aware of their problems, they fail to deal with the issues correctly.

Problems drag on and are made worse by things like credit problems, waiting for payments that never happen, accumulating bills and similar disappointments. Problems compound and multiply. These issues, if they're allowed to continue, resolve themselves into sudden unexpected crises.

Outcomes Other than Voluntary Arrangements

If the business owners don't accept the situation and appoint an insolvency practitioner to discuss a voluntary arrangement, the options are

- *Receivership*: A receivership is when a bank appoints a receiver to sell the assets it has security over. This happens when a business is considered salvageable.
- *Liquidation*: If a business isn't considered salvageable, the business is wound up by either application, by the owners, for voluntary liquidation or liquidation processes conducted by a liquidator appointed either by creditors or a court.

If a creditor obtains a court judgment for an unpaid debt, which then remains unpaid, the creditor can apply for a winding-up order, which can start the liquidation process.

When the business's bankers discover that a winding-up petition has been made, they will freeze the bank account.

This effectively puts the company out of business as it will be unable to pay staff, order supplies or carry on business as usual.

The bankers are required by law to freeze the company bank account.

An insolvent company is legally obligated to cease all financial transactions, and its bank could (and often is) held responsible for any of the company's debts in the period that the bank should have frozen the account.

Examples of Disasters

Large businesses can make disastrous business decisions, as the following examples show.

Ill-conceived forays into areas where the business has no experience can cost the business dearly. Virgin found this out when they decided to enter the soft drinks market and launch Virgin Cola. Even Richard Branson admits that they hadn't thought things through.

Virgin usually only enters a market when they feel that they can give customers something strikingly different, that will disrupt the market. But what Virgin didn't realize was that the consumer was already getting something that they liked, and at a price they were willing to pay. Virgin also underestimated Coca-Cola's aggressive response to the newcomer, and the existing customer loyalty to their brand.

Virgin Cola was not different enough to make a significant impact on the market. They had broken their own rules in entering the soft drinks market, and their failure is an indictment of that.

Coca-Cola isn't immune from bad business though, as their foray into the bottled water market will show.

Coca-Cola were confident that their stylish purified water product Dasani would be a success in the UK. Five years earlier, it had launched the brand in the USA, and they had generated sales of 1.3 billion liters a year.

However, it was a disaster for Coca-Cola, who invested $13 million on the UK launch, when it emerged that the factory in Kent that made Dasani used ordinary tap water as the source.

Also, the local utilities company disclosed that it charged just 0.03p for the same quantity of water as that contained in Dasani's 95p bottle.

In addition, it came to light that the water contained up to 22 μg per liter of bromate, a carcinogen, which is more than double the limit permitted in the EU.

Within weeks of the launch, Dasani was pulled and plans to roll it out in Germany and France were canceled.

Although the foregoing problems were disappointing for the companies involved, they were not disastrous as the businesses are of a size to cope with such disappointments.

Smaller businesses do not have the ability to weather such storms, and should monitor their performance on an ongoing basis to ensure that they are not failing in any way.

Indications of Poor Performance

Indications that your business is not performing well are

1. Poor cash flow
2. Overeagerness to collect customer receipts
3. Sleepless nights worrying about personal guarantees
4. Reluctance to replace assets or invest in the business
5. Being on first name terms with the recoveries department at your bank

6. Devising schemes to delay or avoid payments to the Tax Authorities
7. Canceling expansion plans or new initiatives
8. Aggressive suppliers demanding overdue payments
9. Threats of winding-up petitions
10. Considering redundancy costs

Many businesses have historically carried on trading in difficulty if they have been threatened with bankruptcy/winding-up petitions, in the hope that things will get better, and that they will weather the storm.

But companies that have been served with these notices risk being accused of wrongful trading if they continue to carry on business while insolvent.

Wrongful and Fraudulent Trading

Business owners in this position need to understand the difference between wrongful trading and fraudulent trading. They are quite distinct in terms of law, and one carries much stiffer penalties than the other.

Wrongful trading refers to businesses that continue to carry on their daily business trading while they are insolvent, that is, they are unable to pay their debts as they fall due.

They do this in the hope that things will improve even though they continue to spiral downward.

In wrongful trading there is no intent to defraud the company's creditors but merely a case of poor judgment or the failure of the business owners to carry out their responsibilities.

Fraudulent trading is where the business carries on trading while the business owners have no intention of paying the debts due, and they have the intention of defrauding the creditors of the amounts due to them.

If a business owner is convicted of fraudulent trading, there is a maximum prison sentence of 10 years and/or a fine.

The fraudulent trading penalties do not just apply in insolvent situations, but also where a business has been set up with the sole intention of defrauding its creditors.

As explained in Chapter 3, if an unincorporated business becomes insolvent, the payment of its debts becomes the sole responsibility of the business owner.

True entrepreneurs never seemed fazed when things are going/or have gone badly wrong, as they always seem able or regroup and start all over again. So how do you know when it isn't working and it's time to call it a day?

I could answer this question with the standard reply 'if at first you don't succeed...', but I prefer Winston Churchill's quote: 'Success is the ability to go from one failure to another with no loss of enthusiasm'. So learn from your mistakes and carry on!

Chasing Sales

Businesses can often overstretch themselves to the point where they find themselves reliant upon future income to pay current liabilities and think that they can trade out of the problems. This is often described as 'chasing sales'.

I have seen many businesses in trouble who concentrate too much on creating further sales, while overlooking the fundamental problems that their business has got.

As the business has been built up by an entrepreneur, who in essence is often a salesman, they see more sales as the answer to their problems, and this often isn't the case.

The sooner the business sorts out its fundamental problems the better, so that's where the attention should be focused.

You will have gathered from the above that I have little respect for our banking community. This is because I am aware of at least two bankruptcies that were caused by banks imposing unnecessary financial restructuring upon sound businesses.

The banks gained significantly from their actions, but the interest rate swap scandal is maybe a topic for a further book!

Chapter 11

Retirement and Succession

At some stage, the issue of the business cessation or sale needs to be addressed, and/or the provision for the succession of the next generation needs to be considered.

There are legal issues, the provisions in leases and redundancy payments, for example, that will need to be addressed. There are also the responsibilities to employees, who are reliant upon the business for their and their families lifestyles, to be considered.

Passing the Business on to the Family upon Death or Retirement

The potential problem of passing on the business intact to the family needs to be discussed with legal advisers at an early stage while everyone is in good health and gets on well. How the family each receive an equal share of a business that cannot be easily split is a dilemma that has cost many a business a fortune in legal fees.

For example, a farm because of its acreage will usually have a high asset value. But it will often only generate a small profit. If the farm is the only asset in the deceased's estate, it is often not possible to split the farm and leave a viable business.

This is why there are a large number of farming partnerships, where the farm has not been split between the beneficiaries, who have continued to operate the whole business between themselves.

This can cause problems if the beneficiaries are unable to work together.

The next generation may split into different factions, each with different ideas as to how the business should be run. The question of whether the next generation will be able to work together needs to be addressed.

A further complication with farming businesses is that the main residence is often the farmhouse, which can't be sold and the proceeds split between the beneficiaries without having an impact on the business.

This problem can also impact other businesses outside of farming.

A business owner needs to plan for this problem by investing in other assets outside of the business so that his estate does not comprise solely of his business.

The format of the business may also play a major role in the decision of bequeathing assets to beneficiaries. Whether the business is a sole trader, partnership or limited company can have a major impact on the alternatives available to the business owner, as each offers different opportunities for splitting the business.

Shares in a company can be easily allocated, but the majority shareholding and ultimately the control of the business cannot be gifted lightly.

Splitting up a family business can be a difficult thing. Although it is often easy to split it up into equal shares, it is difficult to forecast which members of the family have the capabilities to take the business forward.

First- and second-generation business owners tend to be more motivated than the third-generation onward, who have grown up with all the benefits that the business has provided, but without the knowledge of how hard they were to achieve.

It is often these third-generation business owners who take less of an interest in the business and employ professional management teams to take things forward.

This approach can have a negative impact on the loyal staff and customers who have grown with the business.

Often, those who inherit a business have careers of their own and have no interest in taking over a venture they have no knowledge of, and they feel that a sale as a going concern is their only option.

Retirement and Pensions

In the previous section, we looked briefly at how a business could be passed on to the family on death or retirement, and highlighted the pitfalls often encountered in this process.

Now it's time to look at retirement from the business owner's perspective.

This section, and those following, look at maximizing the payout you receive at the end of your working life.

Have you asked yourself what you are doing it all for? Do you plan to jet off to the Caribbean while you still have lead in your pencil? Have you planned for the financial resources you will need to do this?

The self-employed have historically been very bad in planning for retirement, often thinking that 'my business is my pension', thinking that they cannot afford to provide for a future that always seems an eternity away.

But putting cash aside is easier than you think, with tax relief available on most forms of savings intended to fund retirement.

Individual Savings Accounts (ISAs)

Self-employed people generally need to keep their finances flexible to cater for any downturns in their earnings, so their savings should not be locked away in pensions.

Instant access ISAs provide this flexibility, in that the saver can have access to their savings at any time that they need them.

There are four types of ISAs:

1. *Cash ISA*: This is basically a savings account with tax-free interest.
2. *Help to buy ISA*: This is basically a savings account as in (1), but it is set up with the main aim of providing a deposit on a first-time residential property. The government provides a 25% boost to the savings in the account.
3. *Innovative finance ISAs*: These are accounts where the savings can be lent to third parties, and the loan interest is received tax-free. The increase in crowdfunding dictated this innovative account.
4. *Stocks and shares ISAs*: The savings can be invested directly into stocks and shares, with the capital gains and dividends being received in the ISA tax-free.

An ISA allowance of £20,000 a year is available to anyone over the age of 16 in the UK, and money within the ISA grows tax-free.

The amount can be split between the different ISAs available, or all can be invested in one.

Savings within an ISA remain tax-free as long as they stay there, and the accumulated ISA allowances, since the ISA was introduced in 1999, mean that £116,000 plus interest could have built up in an ISA started at that date.

The ISA allowance is very flexible; for example, an individual could invest, say, £5,000 in a cash ISA, £10,000 in a stocks and shares ISA and £5,000 in an innovative finance ISA. As long as the combined investment in the year does not exceed £20,000.

Pensions

Given the flexibility of the ISA, pensions should not be ignored as they also benefit from tax relief and the contributions can also bring the investor below certain tax thresholds.

The self-employed are not very good at providing for their retirement. There are around 4.5 million people now working for themselves in the UK, with just 18% of them contributing to a pension. This compares with 48% of those who are employed.

For most self-employed people, the best approach to long-term savings will usually be a mixture of ISAs and pensions.

Increase in the State Pension Age

Many people think that they can rely on the state pension to fund their retirement, but even with a complete national insurance record you can only expect to receive £8000 a year when you retire. You are likely to need far more for a comfortable old age.

Not only is the state pension currently inadequate to provide for a comfortable retirement, but there are plans in place to increase the retirement date over the next few years.

I have included copies of the government's tables showing the effect of these changes (Tables 11.1 through 11.3).

Between October 2018 and October 2020, both men and women's state pension age will increase to 66, and between 2026 and 2028 it will increase again to 67 (Table 11.1)

The changes are aimed at bringing women's state pension age into line with men's, also taking into account that everyone is living longer (Table 11.2).

Table 11.1   Increase in State Pension Age from 65 to 66, Men and Women

Date of Birth	Date State Pension Age Reached
6 December 1953–5 January 1954	6 March 2019
6 January 1954–5 February 1954	6 May 2019
6 February 1954–5 March 1954	6 July 2019
6 March 1954–5 April 1954	6 September 2019
6 April 1954–5 May 1954	6 November 2019
6 May 1954–5 June 1954	6 January 2020
6 June 1954–5 July 1954	6 March 2020
6 July 1954–5 August 1954	6 May 2020
6 August 1954–5 September 1954	6 July 2020
6 September 1954–5 October 1954	6 September 2020
6 October 1954–5 April 1960	66th birthday

There are also plans to increase the retirement age to 68, as can be seen in Table 11.3.

So, there is a real need for business owners to provide for a retirement income for the years prior to the state retirement date, should they wish to retire before then, and also to provide for additional amounts to supplement the state pension once it is received.

But how much should you be saving to provide for a decent retirement?

Most financial advisers suggest that a half to two-thirds of your current income will be enough to meet your needs when you retire, and the earlier you can start saving, the better.

I can show you the importance of starting early in the following calculation:

If an investor started saving £100 a month for 40 years, he would put the same amount into his investment as someone

Table 11.2   Increase in State Pension Age from 66 to 67, Men and Women

Date of Birth	Date State Pension Age Reached
6 April 1960–5 May 1960	66 years and 1 months
6 May 1960–5 June 1960	66 years and 2 months
6 June 1960–5 July 1960	66 years and 3 months
6 July 1960–5 August 1960	66 years and 4 months[a]
6 August 1960–5 September 1960	66 years and 5 months
6 September 1960–5 October 1960	66 years and 6 months
6 October 1960–5 November 1960	66 years and 7 months
6 November 1960–5 December 1960	66 years and 8 months
6 December 1960–5 January 1961	66 years and 9 months[b]
6 January 1961–5 February 1961	66 years and 10 months[c]
6 February 1961–5 March 1961	66 years and 11 months
6 March 1961–5 April 1977*	67

[a] Any person born on 31st July 1960 is considered to reach the age of 66 years and 4 months on 30th November 2026.

[b] Any person born on 31st December 1960 is considered to reach the age of 66 years and 9 months on 30th September 2027.

[c] Any person born on 31st January 1961 is considered to reach the age of 66 years and 10 months on 30th November 2027.

* People born after 5th April 1969, but before 6th April 1977, under the Pensions Act 2007, their Pension age was already agreed to be 67.

starting 20 years later, putting £200 a month in (both investors would have contributed £48,000). If over the period there had been investment growth of 5% a year, the investment over the 40-year period will have accumulated to £148,856.46, while the 20-year investment would total only £81,491.56 (Table 11.3).

The monies invested in personal pensions can be accessed from the age of 55, either through an annuity or by way of income drawdown. Up to 25% of the pension fund can be withdrawn tax-free.

Table 11.3   Increase in State Pension Age from 67 to 68, Men and Women

Date of Birth	Date State Pension Age Reached
6 April 1977–5 May 1977	6 May 2044
6 May 1977–5 June 1977	6 July 2044
6 June 1977–5 July 1977	6 September 2044
6 July 1977–5 August 1977	6 November 2044
6 August 1977–5 September 1977	6 January 2045
6 September 1977–5 October 1977	6 March 2045
6 October 1977–5 November 1977	6 May 2045
6 November 1977–5 December 1977	6 July 2045
6 December 1977–5 January 1978	6 September 2045
6 January 1978–5 February 1978	6 November 2045
6 February 1978–5 March 1978	6 January 2046
6 March 1978–5 April 1978	6 March 2046
6 April 1978 onward	68th birthday

Annuities

An annuity is where the pension pot (usually after the pay-out of the 25% tax-free) is used to buy a fixed income, which will be paid for the rest of the pensioner's life. The amount received will be based on the size of the pension pot and current interest rates, among other things.

Income Drawdown

Income drawdown (more often referred to as drawdown) allows the pensioner to choose and vary the income that they take from their pension pot. The pensioner has the freedom to decide the amount they wish to draw from their funds in order to suit their changing needs.

There are a number of rules and restrictions regarding drawdown, and these vary from company to company.

Annuities Explained Further

Once the annuity has been purchased by the pensioner, the contract is fixed for life, which means that the pensioner will not have to think about their pension arrangements again. It has the benefit that it secures an income for life.

If there are health issues which may result in a reduced life expectancy, this may lead to the annuity rate being increased, in some cases by up to a third.

Insurance companies are not as willing to gamble on life expectancy as they used to be, and the rates offered are currently low. As people are generally living longer, the annuities paid are getting smaller.

The benefits offered by annuity providers can vary enormously so it is worth shopping around for the best deal. The annuity rates offered can vary, and some providers offer a number of benefits, which can include a small amount of life cover in the early years of the arrangement.

Given that the whole pot is exchanged for the promised annuity, it is relatively easy to calculate the payback period and compare it with your life expectancy to calculate whether you are getting a good deal.

The following table shows the annuity rates currently being offered (2017). As you can see, they vary with age, and some offer a guarantee of the amount, and an escalation to cope with inflationary factors.

Age	Level Rate No Guarantee	Level Rate+ 10-year Guarantee	3% Escalation No Guarantee
65	£5203	£5131	£3577
70	£5928	£5823	£4349
75	£7118	£6821	£5303

These figures are based on a pension pot of £100,000; therefore, a 75-year-old taking the level rate, no guarantee option would have to live for 14 years to get his money back (i.e., £100,000/£7,118 = 14.05).

Once the annuity is purchased, the pensioner has the option to reinvest small amounts (from the 25% tax-free) back into the fund to increase the annuity being received.

Annuities tend to be fairly inflexible once the annuity rate has been agreed and purchased.

Once you buy an annuity, you need to realize that your pension pot has gone, and should you die a short time thereafter there will be nothing left to leave to your family.

The current government has suggested that it would introduce legislation allowing pensioners to sell their annuities (if they were not happy with them) in exchange for a lump sum, but it has since reversed its policy.

Drawdown Explained Further

If you opt for drawdown, you can have unrestricted access to your pension pot, which gives you the financial flexibility to deal with all that life throws at you.

The main advantage that drawdown has over annuities is that you always have access to your pension pot, and upon death, before the age of 75, that pot is still available for your family to inherit tax-free.

After the age of 75, the family would have to pay tax on the value of the undrawn pot at that date.

With drawdown giving pensioners access to their pension pot, they can often land themselves in financial difficulty by making poor decisions when withdrawing their funds.

Tax Relief on Pension Contributions

Tax relief is given on pension contributions at the rate of tax that the taxpayer is subject to. For example, a basic rate taxpayer, making a £100 pension contribution will pay just £80, as the pension company will claim the tax relief directly.

It is slightly more complicated for higher rate and additional rate taxpayers, as they will need to claim the additional 20% and 25% on their tax returns, making their net costs £60 and £55.

Generally speaking, total annual contributions to a pension policy are limited to your income – which does not include dividends – or the Annual Allowance of £40,000, whichever is the lower.

Also, provided that the total contribution does not exceed these limits, your limited company can make pension contributions and deduct them as a cost against its corporation tax bill.

Growth within the pension fund is free of income tax and capital gains, and the first 25% lump sum you can take at age 55 is tax-free too. Pension funds are also tax-free for your beneficiaries if you die before retirement.

Tax on pensions is very complicated, and advice should be sought before any action is taken.

Different Types of Pensions

The main types of pensions available to business owners are stakeholder pensions and self-invested personal pensions (SIPPs). The differences between the two are mainly due to (1) the charges payable to the pension providers, (2) the flexibility regarding the savings and (3) the investment choices available.

Stakeholder pensions. These must meet minimum standards set by the government regarding limited charges, low minimum and flexible contributions, charge-free transfers and a default investment fund for those who do not want to choose a specific fund.

SIPPs. These are seen as the default pension choice for many self-employed people as they are very flexible regarding the investments they can hold.

This can sometimes include the business's commercial premises, which can allow for some tax-efficient arrangements regarding rentals and sales.

However, nothing ever comes for free, and the fees charged by SIPP administrators verge on extortion in some cases. It is a sector full of greedy administrators who have little regard for their clients.

I include the foregoing caveat as a warning for you to avoid any tax saving scheme as the main beneficiary will usually be the SIPP provider.

Financial Advisors

There are many financial advisors around who are desperate to advise people on their savings and investments, and my attitude to them has always been 'if you were really good at what you are doing you wouldn't be working for a living'.

Choosing the right advisor is nearly as hard as choosing the right savings program for yourself. How do you know you are getting the best advice from your advisor, or are they pocketing huge commissions from your investments? Unfortunately, it is often too late before you find the answer to that question.

A lot of regulations have been introduced in the financial services sector, but the rogues still persist. In addition, the larger businesses in this sector tend to be very good at following the rules and completing all the statutory paperwork, but their intentions have proved to be anything but true.

They are compliant in regard to the paperwork but still have little regard to their ultimate purpose, which is to provide decent pensions for their clients.

NEST

You can't go far wrong by trusting your future to the National Employment Savings Trust (NEST), which was set up by the government as an auto-enrolment scheme primarily for the benefit of employees.

NEST accepts self-employed people as well as employees, and only charges around 0.5%, which is significantly lower than the amounts charged to most stakeholder schemes (which are currently limited to 1.5%).

NEST offers five investment funds to choose from, designed to match the investor's attitude to risk. If these funds do not provide what you are after, there are hundreds of others available in the pensions offered by providers such as Standard Life, Legal and General, etc.

Old Pensions

If, before you became self-employed, you had an old pension pot which you contributed to in a previous employment, you will have the choice of leaving it as a paid-up fund, contributing further amounts to it or transferring the balance to any new fund you are setting up.

If your former employer has negotiated good terms with the pension provider, it may be better to leave it where it is.

Or, you may prefer to transfer the amount to the new pension scheme that you are setting up.

A review of the transfer fees that may be payable on any transfer to a new fund may sway your decision on that course of action. Some companies can charge up to 100% of the fund value!

What Is the Best Retirement Date?

There is no date within a tax year which would provide an optimum tax saving upon retirement, so you should retire on the date most suited to you, although purely from a tax administration point of view, the end of a tax year would be the most convenient.

Retirement on any date after March will result in the necessity to file an income tax return for the following year.

There is a complication, however, which may affect individuals retiring from businesses with other than March year-ends. Additional tax may be payable by those individuals in their retirement year as a result of the closing year rules basis of assessment.

These rules are quite complex, and I don't intend to explain them fully in this book. Suffice to say that where these rules do apply, more than 12 months profits will be taxed in the final year in business.

There is no way to avoid the rules by retiring on a specific date within that final year. The Tax Authorities allow a credit against the extra tax liability by way of a claim for 'overlap relief', although the longer that the individual has been in business, the less the value of that credit will be.

Remember, you can start taking the benefits from your pension scheme from age 55, even if you don't retire.

Investing in Someone Else's Business: What to Expect

Most small businesses are owned by the founding entrepreneur, his or her family members and/or a few investing partners, and most will raise funds using established routes such as bankers, etc.

Crowdfunding has provided an opportunity for those businesses not only to look at other ways of raising funds but also for investors to take shares in those small businesses.

Prior to this, the only way that most investors could invest in businesses was by purchasing shares of companies listed on stock exchanges, such as the Dow Jones, the FTSE100 and the Nasdaq.

I referred previously to 'most' investors, as there has always been a route for angel investors to take investments (and often a limited management role) in fledgling businesses, and an active market for venture capitalist firms to take shares in businesses which they consider to be good long-term investments.

If we take into account the fact that most people have not got the access and connections that venture capital firms possess, the opportunities left are for investment via crowdfunding or the angel investor route.

If the crowdfunding option is taken, it is basically an arm's length investment with no active participation in the operations or decision-making of the business, and much the same as owning shares in a public quoted company.

The crowdfunding option allows the investor to invest from as little as £10 to as much as they like.

The angel investor route will usually involve an investment in a small or family-owned business, and the investment may come with a job in the management of the business.

The investor, usually making a significant investment, may be expected to participate as a member of the business's management team, usually the board of directors, to advise on the policies and direction of the business.

What Are You Looking for from the Investment?

If you are looking for a challenge and an active role in a business, you can discount the crowdfunding option and actively look for a business that could benefit from your input.

As you are looking to participate in the business, you will need to find one local to you, and make your wishes known to professionals such as bank managers, accountants and solicitors in your area.

They can then act as matchmaker and organize introductions to potential candidate businesses.

Your expectations regarding the level of active involvement and income will dictate which candidates will be the most appropriate.

How Much to Invest?

Are you looking for a minor position within a business to keep you active, or are you looking to take over a business you feel could do better. The capital you will need to input would differ significantly between these two options.

Are your pension funds insufficient to provide you with your planned retirement, and are you looking for further growth in that value from your investment? Then you need to examine in detail the business you are considering investing in, as each comes with its own rewards.

Startups: Tend to be high risk with no management track record or proven business model, and often require more input to keep them afloat. Startups would not be advised as a place to invest a retirement fund.

As already discussed, there is a very high failure rate of startup businesses, but businesses such as Microsoft, Google, Amazon and Apple were initially startups.

Second-level capital acquisitions: These are companies that have got off the ground with the capital input by the founders, but now need more capital to grow. These companies have a performance record and are usually less risky than startups.

Turnaround companies: These are businesses which are in failure mode and require an improvement of management and finances to turn them around.

Often, the cash flow and the business model and fundamentals are good, but bad management decisions have left the business in a precarious position.

All the business needs is new management and an input of finance. But note, if the cash flow and fundamentals are bad, the prospects for recovery will be extremely limited.

Successful turnarounds can offer a high return on investment.

Growth opportunity: These are businesses whose growth has been held back by a lack of capital, and they may be a good investment target if their fundamentals, track record and management are capable of handling further growth.

Bankrupt: These are businesses that can provide great value at a low price, if the reasons for the bankruptcy can be identified and overcome.

It may have been bad management or lack of expense control, and if these issues can be dealt with a phoenix could arise from the ashes.

This is a high-risk investment that may require high personal involvement, and it could be either very lucrative or devastating for the investor.

The Pros and Cons of Investing in Privately Owned Businesses

The pros of investing in privately owned businesses are as follows:

■ You can agree your input in terms of finance and personal involvement, and set your goal in terms of the return you want on your investment.
■ You can also agree an exit plan once an agreed goal has been achieved, and structure payments etc. to suit your tax needs.
■ Smaller businesses are easier to work with and to allow the investor to build up a relationship with the management team.

- Smaller businesses offer the chance of more spectacular growth.
- The financial information of a smaller business is relatively easy to understand.
- As a significant investor in a smaller business, you are more likely to be able to influence operational decisions.
- There is less of a market to provide finance and advice to a smaller business, and that reduced competition means the investor will be highly considered by the management.

The cons of investing in privately owned businesses are as follows:

- It is difficult to obtain comparative performance data and industry benchmarks for smaller businesses.
- Smaller businesses have less rigorous accounting, reporting and transparency standards than those required of publicly traded companies.
- Often, the founder will not have the skills to continue running the business at the current stage of its development, and will not be willing to accept their shortcomings.
- Smaller businesses may find it difficult to raise finance.
- Smaller family businesses can face issues such as succession (discussed at the start of this chapter).
- As a minority investor, you may have a small amount of influence on policy decisions.
- The business needs to carefully plan for cash flow to enable a payout of the investment at a later date.

One of the most successful investments I have seen an entrepreneur make was quite a brave one in a business set up by two ex-employees.

The entrepreneur had identified the abilities of the employees and offered them management roles within his own business. The employees turned the offer down, as they wanted something inherently theirs.

The business reluctantly let the employees go, and assisted them in setting up their own business, in competition to themselves. They also provided a small amount of capital to help the startup.

The two businesses then began a close working relationship, which resulted in them controlling their market between themselves.

What could have been a conflict with strained relations between the two, ended up as a very successful enterprise.

Does this bear any similarity to the Starbucks example in Chapter 1?

When considering an investment in a small business, a lot of work is needed to research the target company carefully, including financial reports, bank statements, market niche, competition, management skill levels and track record, cost trends as a percentage of revenues, the principal relationships and why the company needs the investment.

If it all looks good, keep the investment small enough to preserve your portfolio diversity. If you are a minority investor, with or without board or management participation, it is useful to know the business owners well. If you do your homework, there is money to be made investing in small businesses.

Chapter 12

Essentials to Take Away

The Customer Should Always Come First

The customer should always come first. You need to ensure that they are never made feel like a nuisance. You need to welcome them and make their experience a pleasure that they look forward to.

Never quibble with them regarding their displeasure, as the goodwill lost will cost more than the product with which they are unhappy. Pick your customers carefully, so disputes should be few and far between.

Personal Complaints Line

You should provide a personal complaints line direct to yourself. The customer will appreciate the personal service from the boss, and if you are doing things right it shouldn't be a time-consuming task.

This also ensures that your staff are unable to hide customer dissatisfaction from you. It will give you an insight into what's really going on. The buck should stop with you anyway.

Be the Best

Be the best, don't accept second rate because your customers won't. You need to instill this attitude in your staff.

Keep an eye on your competitors and focus on how you can do it better. Match them on any improvements they are making in dealing with their customers.

Incorporate

Incorporate your business to limit your liabilities. If your incorporated business fails, all is not lost.

By incorporating, you will get access to higher-quality advisors who don't tend to advise sole traders and other small entities.

It's a Team

Work with your partners and staff as a team, and pool resources and skills. Your staff need to know that the happier customers are, the more salary they will receive.

The achievements that the business makes should be celebrated with the team of staff that are responsible for them.

Don't Have a Plan B

Having a plan B takes away the focus from plan A. Having a plan B is accepting that plan A may not work.

It'll Work... Think Positively

Train yourself to disregard your negativity. Think positively and have a half-full attitude.

Believe in yourself and don't let anyone undermine your confidence.

All groundbreakers have had to fight a lot of negativity to achieve what they have. If you can't do this, how can you expect your team to believe in you.

Don't Ever Assume Things

Don't assume that everyone sees the world as you see it, especially your customers. Try to see their experience through their eyes.

Don't assume that your customers are happy because they don't complain, and then review the amount of times that you have assumed that someone else will complain about something that you haven't complained about.

Attention to Detail

Pay attention to detail, as little things mean a lot. You don't get a second chance to make a first impression.

Small details such as flowers and up-to-date magazines in reception, to uniforms and general staff appearance, and biscuits with the coffee provided can distinguish you from your competitors.

React to Change

Be able to react to change, and be innovative. But try to be proactive rather than reactive. Don't get stuck in your ways and insist that your business is better than the usurpers.

Don't Ignore the Financials

Don't ignore the financials, keep an eye on your budgets. Have a plan and review progress and reassess whether your targets are going to get you to where you want to be.

Do It for Yourself

When you stop jumping out of bed eager for work, have a rethink at what you're doing and why.

Have fun, don't let it take over your life entirely. Take time out to do what you want with your life. Don't get trapped having to work to pay off a mortgage on a property you don't really need.

Plan for retirement, you can't do it forever, and remember that there ain't no pockets in shrouds.

Or the stress will kill you eventually.

Take Advice

Take advice from professionals and follow it. Ignore what it says on Google, professional advisors do know what they're talking about (mostly!).

Get Insured

Ensure you are insured for all eventualities (because they do happen!), then forget about it.

Insure the lifestyle that you want for the rest of your life.

You've got a responsibility to your employees to ensure their lifestyles also.

Start Your Pension Early

The earlier you start to build your pension pot, the bigger it will grow. You're likely to outlive your pension pot because we're all living longer!

What Makes a Successful Business?

Luck, good judgment and a lot of hard work.

Business Plan

A well thought-through business plan is essential for a successful business. I include an example of a business plan next as an indication of the detail that is usual in such a document.

Example of a Business Plan/Finance Application

BUSINESS PLAN FOR JT'S RESTAURANT.
                                        AUGUST 2017

Index
  Summary of Application
  Financial statements of Yoko's Sushi House (only one year included here)
  Resumes of Paul Kendall and Tony Zoyo (not included in this book)
  Details of profit shares and ownership from years 1 to 5 (not included)
  Details of profit shares and ownership for years 6 to 10 (not included)
  Financial forecasts of JT's Restaurant to 30 June 2020 (included in Chapter 3)
  Draft agreement to sell the property to be known as JT's Restaurant at a fixed price of £200,000 in five years' time (not included)

Detailed breakdown of the purchase price of £120,000 (not included)

Valuations and details of inventory (not included)

BUSINESS PLAN FOR JT'S RESTAURANT.

AUGUST 2017

Summary of Application

The following detail lays out Paul Kendall's and Tony Zoyo's (otherwise known as Japanese Tony or JT) plans to set up a business called JT's Restaurant, based in the premises previously known as Yoko's Sushi House in Birmington, UK, on 1 July 2017.

The audited accounting records of Yoko's Sushi House for the three years to March 2016 are appended to this document (on the understanding that the detail therein is confidential and disclosed solely for the purpose of this finance application (Table 12.1)).

Paul Kendall is a retired chartered accountant and is to undertake a management and administrative position in the business (for tax and security reasons the business is to be set up as a sole trader in his name).

Tony Zoyo is a very experienced chef, who has worked in a number of Michelin-starred restaurants, and for a time in Yoko's Sushi House.

The resumes of both of the above are appended to this document.

The plan is to buy the business (only) of Yoko's Sushi House, as the present owners want to retain the property (initially). It will become available for sale after year five, the owners' reasons for this delay are not known at this stage (but it may be due to taxation).

It has been agreed that the property will be sold to Tony for a fixed price of £200,000 in five years' time, and further funding may be required at that stage if the business hasn't built up a reserve of retained profits at that point.

The association between Paul and Tony needs further explanation in order to assist with this finance application. They have known each other for a number of years and Paul is a regular customer at the restaurant.

The owners have made it known that they wish to retire from the business, and Tony, who has put in a lot of effort to make the business what it is today, does not want to see his efforts wasted.

He has negotiated the purchase price of the business using his personal relationship with the current owners, and the price would be far higher on the open market.

Unfortunately, due to events outside of Tony's control, Tony's finances are far from ideal to apply for a business loan.

Paul has a lot of faith in Tony's culinary skills, and is willing to put security up and provide management expertise to help Tony take over the business.

In exchange for this, Tony has agreed to fix his income from the business to a salary of £60,000 a year for the first five years, and has agreed to Paul's staggered withdrawal from the business thereafter.

They have decided to change the business name as they wanted it known that Tony will have more of an active role in the business, and his culinary skills and involvement will be focused on.

Financial forecasts for the first three years trading of JT's Restaurant are appended to this document, and are very much in line with the business's current trading.

(Example of statutory accounts)
**Yoko's Sushi House Limited
Directors' Report and Unaudited
Financial Statements**

For the year ended 31 March 2014

**Yoko's Sushi House Limited
Company information
31 March 2014**

Directors	Yoko Fernandez
	Rafa Fernandez
Company Number	12345678
Registered Office	The Sushi House
	Winkle Street
	Birmington
	BE1 1EZ
	UK
Accountants	Fiddle & Scarper
	Balance House
	Money Lane
	Birmington
	BE1 1EL
	UK

Yoko's Sushi House Limited

Directors' Report
For the year ended 31 March 2014
The directors present their report and financial statements for the year ended 31 March 2014.

Principal Activities
The principal activity of the company was that of a licensed restaurant.

Directors
The following directors have held office since 1 April 2013:

Mr. R. Fernandez
Mrs. Y. Fernandez

This report has been prepared in accordance with the special provisions relating to small companies within Part 15 of the Companies Act 2006

On behalf of the board

Mr. R. Fernandez
30 September 2014

Yoko's Sushi House Limited
Chartered Accountants Report to the Board of
Directors on the preparation of the unaudited
Statutory Financial Statements of Yoko's Sushi House
Limited for the year ended 31 March 2014

In order to assist you to fulfil your duties under the Companies Act 2006, we have prepared for your approval the financial statements of Yoko' Sushi House Limited for the year ended 31 March 2014, set out on pages 3 to 10, from the company's accounting records, and from information and explanations you have given us.

As a practicing member firm of the Institute of Chartered Accountants in England and Wales, we are subject to its ethical and other professional requirements which are detailed at icaew.com/regulations.

This report is made solely to the Board of Directors of Yoko's Sushi House Limited as a body, in accordance with the terms of our engagement letter dated 11 June 2013.

Our work has been undertaken solely to prepare for your approval the financial statements of Yoko's Sushi House Limited and state those matters that we have agreed to state to the Board of Directors of Yoko's Sushi House Limited as a body, in this report in accordance with AAF 2/10 as detailed at icaew.com/compilation.

To the fullest extent permitted by law, we do not accept or assume responsibility to anyone other than Yoko's Sushi House Limited and its Board of Directors as a body, for our work or this report.

It is your duty to ensure that Yoko's Sushi House Limited has kept adequate accounting records and to prepare statutory financial statements that give a true and fair view of the assets, liabilities, financial position and profit of Yoko's Sushi House Limited.

You consider that Yoko's Sushi House Limited is exempt from the statutory audit requirement for the year.

We have not been instructed to carry out an audit or a review of the financial statements of Yoko's Sushi House Limited. For this reason, we have not verified the accuracy or completeness of the accounting records or information and explanations you have given to us and we do not, therefore, express any opinion on the statutory financial statements.

Fiddle & Scarper
Balance House
Birmington
30 September 2014

Yoko's Sushi House Limited
Profit and Loss account
For the Year Ended 31 March 2014

	Notes	£
Turnover		182,296
Cost of sales		(55,162)
Gross Profit		127,134
Administrative expenses		(95,312)
Operating profit	2.	31,822
Other interest receivable and similar income	3.	70
Profit on ordinary activities		
Before taxation		31,892
Tax on ordinary activities	4.	(14,703)
Profit for the year	11.	17,189

Yoko's Sushi House Limited
Balance Sheet
As at 31 March 2014

	Notes	£	£
Fixed assets			
Intangible assets	5.		16,000
Tangible assets	6.		<u>39,931</u>
			55,931
Current assets			
Stocks		4,568	
Debtors	7.	330	
Cash at bank and in hand		<u>5,191</u>	
		10,089	
Creditors: Amounts falling due within one year	8.	(41,203)	
Net current liabilities			<u>(31,114)</u>
Total assets less current liabilities			24,817
Provision for liabilities	9.		<u>(7,528)</u>
			<u>17,289</u>
Capital and reserves			
Called up share capital	10.		100
Profit and loss account	11.		<u>17,189</u>
Shareholders' funds			<u>17,289</u>

For the financial year ended 31 March 2014, the company was entitled to exemption from audit under Section 477 of the Companies Act 2006 relating to small companies.

Directors responsibilities:

The members have not required the company to obtain an audit of its financial statements for the year in question in accordance with Section 476.

The directors acknowledge their responsibilities for complying with the requirements of the Act with respect to accounting records and the preparation of financial statements.

These financial statements have been prepared in accordance with the provisions applicable to companies subject to the small companies regime and the Financial Reporting Standard for Smaller Entities (effective April 2008).

Approved by the board for issue on

Signed ...., ...

          Director   **Director**

Yoko's Sushi House Limited
Notes to the Financial Statements
For the year ended 31 March 2014

1. ACCOUNTING POLICIES

1.1 Accounting convention

The financial statements are prepared under the historical cost convention and in accordance with the Financial Reporting Standard for Smaller Entities (effective April 2008).

1.2 Compliance with accounting standards

The financial statements are prepared in accordance with applicable United Kingdom Accounting Standards (United Kingdom Generally Accepted Accounting Practice), which have been applied consistently (except as otherwise stated).

1.3 Turnover

Turnover represents the amounts receivable for goods and services net of VAT and trade discounts, to the extent that the company has a right to consideration arising from the performance of its contractual arrangements.

1.4 Goodwill

Acquired goodwill is written off in equal annual instalments over its estimated useful economic life.

Goodwill   -5 years

1.5 Tangible fixed assets and depreciation

Tangible fixed assets are stated at cost less depreciation. Depreciation is provided at rates calculated to write off the cost less the estimated residual value of each asset over its expected useful life, as follows:
   Fixtures, fittings and equipment. Reducing balance 10%

1.6 Stock

Stock is valued at the lower of cost and net realizable value.

1.7 Financial instruments

Financial instruments are classified and accounted for, according to the substance of the contractual arrangement, as either financial assets, financial liabilities or equity instruments. An equity instrument is any contract that evidences a residual interest in the assets of the company after deducting all of its liabilities

1.8 Deferred taxation

Deferred taxation is provided at the appropriate rates on all timing differences using the liability method only to the extent that, in the opinion of the directors, there is a realistic probability that an asset or liability will crystallize in the foreseeable future.

Yoko's Sushi House Limited
Notes to the financial statements (continued)
For the year ended 31 March 2014

2. OPERATING PROFIT

	£
Operating profit is stated after charging:	
Amortization of intangible assets	4000
Depreciation of tangible assets	4133
Directors remuneration	7692

3. INVESTMENT INCOME

	£
Bank interest	70

4. TAXATION

	£
UK corporation tax	7,175
Deferred Tax	7,528
	14,703

5. INTANGIBLE FIXED ASSETS. GOODWILL

	£
Cost	
1 April 2013	20,000
As at 31 March 2014	20,000
Amortization	
As at 1 April 2013	0
Charge for the year	4,000
As at 31 March 2014	4,000
Net book value	
31 March 2014	16,000

Yoko's Sushi House Limited
Notes to the financial statements (continued)
For the year ended 31 March 2014

6. TANGIBLE FIXED ASSETS. FIXTURES, FITTINGS AND EQUIPMENT

	£
Cost	
As at 1 April 2013	0
Additions	44,064
As at 31 March 2014	44,064
Depreciation	
As at 1 April 2013	0
Charge for the year	4,133
As at 31 March 2014	4,133
Net book value	
As at 31 March 2014	39,931

7. DEBTORS

	£
Prepayments and accrued income	330

8. CREDITORS: AMOUNTS FALLING DUE WITHIN ONE YEAR

	£
Bank loans and overdrafts	1,237
Corporation tax	7,175
Other taxes and social security costs	2,093
Directors current accounts	28,930
Accruals and deferred income	1,768
	41,203

Yoko's Sushi House Limited
Notes to the financial statements (continued)
For the year ended 31 March 2014

9. PROVISION FOR LIABILITIES

	Deferred Tax Liability
Accelerated capital allowances	<u>7528</u>

10. SHARE CAPITAL

	£
Allotted, called up and fully paid	
50 A Ordinary shares of £1 each	50
50 B Ordinary shares of £1 each	<u>50</u>
	<u>100</u>

11. STATEMENT OF MOVEMENT ON PROFIT AND LOSS ACCOUNT

	Profit and Loss Account
	£
Profit for the year	<u>17,189</u>

12. CONTROL

The company is controlled jointly by Mr. R. Fernandez and Mrs. Y. Fernandez, who each own a 50% shareholding.

13. RELATED PARTY TRANSACTIONS AND RELATIONSHIPS

Mr. R. Fernandez and Mrs. Y. Fernandez, directors of the company, have a loan account with the company against which personal expenses and drawings may be charged. The loan account has remained in credit throughout the year and the balance at 31 March 2014 was £28,930. The loan is interest free and repayable on demand.

Yoko's Sushi House Limited
Detailed trading and profit and loss account
For the year ended 31 March 2014

	£	£
Turnover		
Sales		182,296
Cost of sales		
Purchases	59,730	
Closing stock	(4,568)	
		55,162
Gross profit		69.74%
		127,134
Administrative expenses		(95,312)
Operating profit		31,822
Other interest receivable		
And similar income		
Bank interest received		70
Profit before taxation		17.49%
		31,892

Yoko's Sushi House Limited
Schedule of administrative expenses
For the year ended 31 March 2014
Administrative expenses

	£
Wages and salaries (excl. NI)	50,432
Directors remuneration	7,692
Employers NI contributions	2,915
Rates	8,021
Insurance	1,004
Light and heat	2,916
Repairs and maintenance	5,267
Printing, postage and stationery	135
Advertising	536
Telephone	1,218
Motor running costs	1,776
Traveling expenses	90
Legal and professional fees	1,408
Accountancy fees	1,400
Bank charges	348
Sundry expenses	2,021
Amortization on goodwill	4,000
Depreciation on fixtures, fittings and equipment	4,133
Total	95,312

Table 12.1 Spreadsheet showing the workings for the tax saving example

Restatement of the company profits

	Three	Two	One
2500 * 12 drawings	30000.00	24000.00	20400.00
Cash excess per calc	69689.00	52999.00	33159.00
Tony's salary add back	60000.00	60000.00	60000.00
	159689.00	136999.00	113559.00
Less paul's salary	66689.00	43999.00	20559.00
Tony's salary	27000.00	27000.00	27000.00
Adjusted company profit	66000.00	66000.00	66000.00
Ct tax @20%	13200.00	13200.00	13200.00
Paul's taxable income	99689.00	76999.00	53559.00
Personal allowances	11500.00	11500.00	11500.00
Net taxable	88189.00	65499.00	42059.00
Basic rate 20%	32000.00	32000.00	32000.00
Higher rate 40%	56189.00	33499.00	10059.00
Tax 20%	6400.00	6400.00	6400.00
40%	22475.60	13399.60	4023.60
Total	28875.60	19799.60	10423.60
Tony's taxable income	60000.00	60000.00	60000.00
Personal allowances	11500.00	11500.00	11500.00
Net taxable	48500.00	48500.00	48500.00
Basic rate 20%	32000.00	32000.00	32000.00
Higher rate 40%	16500.00	16500.00	16500.00
Tax 20%	6400.00	6400.00	6400.00
40%	6600.00	6600.00	6600.00
	13000.00	13000.00	13000.00

Calculation of salaries

Yrs	Paul	2@16500	Net
1	53559.00	33000.00	20559.00
2	76999.00	33000.00	43999.00
3	99689.00	33000.00	66689.00

Yrs	Tony	2@16500	Net
1	60000.00	33000.00	27000.00
2	60000.00	33000.00	27000.00
3	60000.00	33000.00	27000.00

	Yr 1			Yr 2			Yr 3		
Paul's tax salary	20559.00			43999.00			66689.00		
Dividends	16500.00			16500.00			16500.00		
Taxable income	37059.00			60499.00			83189.00		
Personal allow	11500.00			11500.00			11500.00		
Taxable	25559.00			48999.00			71689.00		
Salary	9059.00	20.00%	1811.80	32499.00	20.00%	6499.80	33500.00	20.00%	6700.00
40%							21689.00	40.00%	8675.00
Balance of dividends	11500.00	7.50%	862.50	11500.00	32.50%	3737.50	11500.00	32.50%	3737.50
Dividends	5000.00			5000.00			5000.00		
Nb 1st 5000 tax free	-5000.00		0.00	-5000.00		0.00	-5000.00		0.00
Total tax			2674.30			10237.30			19112.50

Tony's

Salary	27000.00	
Dividends	16500.00	
Taxable income	43500.00	
Personal allow	11500.00	
Taxable	32000.00	
	6400.00	Each year

Index

The 3M Company, *see* Minnesota,
    Mining and Manufacturing
    Company

ACCA, *see* Association of Certified
    Accountants (ACCA)
Accountancy, 126–127, 169
Accountants, 169–171
  expecting from, 171
  finding, 169–171
Accounting convention, 263
Accounting standards, 263
Accounts, 115–173
  accountants, 169–171
    expecting from, 171
    finding, 169–171
  annual review meeting, 172–173
  balance sheet, 130
  bookkeeping and management,
    119–121
  fixed assets, 131
  goodwill, 131–133
    valuations, 132–133
  inspection, 54–55
  legal advisors, 172
    expecting from, 172
    knowledgeable, 172
  level of profit, 128
  need to prepare, 115–116

profit and loss, 121–128
  expenses, 123–128
  income, 121
property, 133–169
  annual percentage rate,
    159–164
  basis of valuation, 144
  critical illness and health
    insurance, 145–147
  current assets, 149–153
  current liabilities, 154–155
  finance/refinance, 141–143
  fixtures and equipment,
    147–148
  freehold *vs.* leasehold,
    135–138
  funding of business accounts,
    164–169
  life insurance and
    endowments, 144–145
  long-term liabilities,
    155–156
  motor vehicles, 148–149
  negative equity and
    valuations, 143
  net assets, 164
  ownership agreement,
    140–141
  owning, 140

purchase of assets and
equipment, 156–158
sale and leaseback, 138–140
type, 134–135
protecting income, 128–129
records, 116–119
tax enquiries, 129–130
Accruals, 154
Adidas, 21
Administrative expenses, 270
Advertising, 126, 180–181
Agricultural relief, 113
American Association for Critical
Illness Insurance, 146
Amron, Alan, 15
Angel investor, 243
Annual Exempt Amount, 105
Annual percentage rate (APR),
159–164
on payday loans, 162–164
working out leasing deal,
160–162
Annual review meeting, 172–173
Annual tax on enveloped dwellings
(ATED), 106–107
Annuities, 236, 237–238
Apple, 9–10
APR, *see* Annual percentage
rate (APR)
Assets
and equipment purchase, 156–158
hire purchase agreement, 157
lease payments, 157–158
own cash, 156
unsecured loan, 156–157
realization of, 215–216
Associated creditors, 211–215
Association of Certified Accountants
(ACCA), 170
Atari, 9
ATED, *see* Annual tax on enveloped
dwellings (ATED)
AuctionWeb, 6

Bad credit control, 199
Bad debts, 151
Balance sheet, 130, 261
Bank account balance, 153
Bank borrowing, 49
Bank charges, 127
Bankers, greedy, 201
Bank loan interest, 128
Bank overdraft, 154
Bankruptcies, 199, 245
Bank statements, 117
Barings Bank, 201
Basic partnership, 31–32
Benchmarking, 170
Blogging, 180
BOGOF, *see* Buy one get one
free (BOGOF)
Bookkeeping and management,
119–121
Brand and logo, 26–27
Branson, Richard, 224
Bridgewater Associates, 71
Budgeting and cash flow, 33–39
Business, 11–24, 11–24
accounts funding, 164–169
capital, 166–167
current, 167–168
drawings and payment of tax,
168–169
brand and logo, 26–27
buying and selling, 43–64
accounts inspection, 54–55
crowdfunding, 52–53
Enterprise Investment Scheme
(EIS), 60–62
finance, 49–52
franchise business, 55–56
incorporated business, 59–60
limited company, 58–59
outlook, 57–58
purchase price, 45–47, 57
sales price, 59
sales split, 58

tax issues, 54
transfer, 47–48
value-added tax (VAT),
47–48
chasing sales, 227–228
company name, 23–24
design, 26–27
disastrous decisions,
224–225
essentials, 249–255
assuming things, 251
attention to detail, 251
customer, 249
get insured, 252
ignoring financials, 252
improvements, 250
incorporation, 250
making successful business, 253
partners and staff as team, 250
personal complaints line, 249
plan, 250, 253–255
react to change, 251
start pension early, 253
stress, 252
take advice, 252
think positively, 250–251
expenses, 118, 129
failures, 200–201
formats, 18–19
unique selling point (USP),
18–19
fraudulent trading, 226–227
growth opportunity, 245
limited company, 29–30
location, 19–20
model and budget, 78, 79,
200–201
partnerships, 21–23, 31–33
Dassler Brothers Sports Shoe
Company, 21
working as team, 22–23
plan, 16, 25–26, 39, 200–201
poor performance, 225–226

pricing and costings, 39–41
promoting, 175–188
advertising, 180–181
blogging, 180
contests and free gifts, 182
discounts, 187
e-mail campaigns, 179
geo-marketing, 184–185
impulse buying, 185–186
joint marketing, 182–183
mailings, 178
marketing methods, 183–184
networking, 187–188
press releases, 180
push and pull marketing,
186–187
return on investment,
177–178
social media, 179
sponsorship and publicity
stunts, 181–182
subcontract web content, 181
website, 175–177
purchase, 171
setting up, 11–18
budgeting and cash flow,
33–39
developing idea, 16–18
evolution, 12–13
opportunity, 13–14
plan, 25–26, 39
Post-it note, 14–15
technological developments,
15–16
unemployment//redundancy, 13
Velcro, 15
Viagra, 12
sole trader approach, 28–29
successful, 189–196
cost cutting, 192–193
extra outlets, 189–190
fine-tuning, 191
franchising, 190

sales promotions and
    marketing campaigns,
    193–196
  time to bring, 20
  wrongful trading, 226–227
Business Relief, 112
Buying and selling, of business,
    43–64
  accounts inspection, 54–55
  crowdfunding, 52–53
  Enterprise Investment Scheme
    (EIS), 60–62
  finance, 49–52
  franchise business, 55–56
  incorporated business, 59–60
  limited company, 58–59
  outlook, 57–58
  purchase price, 45–47
  sales price, 59
  sales split, 58
  tax issues, 54
  transfer, 47–48
  value-added tax (VAT), 47–48
Buy one get one free (BOGOF), 193

Campaign Monitor, 179
Capital accounts, 165, 166–167
Capital allowances, 110
Capital gains tax (CGT), 62,
    103–106
  for people non-domiciled in
    UK, 106
  rates and bands, 105
  rules, 104–105
Capital Gains Tax Deferral Relief,
    62, 64
Cash ISA, 232
Certified Public Accountants
    Institute, 170
CGT, *see* Capital gains tax (CGT)
Chartered accountants report,
    258–259
Chasing sales, 227–228

Checkbooks, 117
Churchill, Winston, 227
Coaching and mentoring, 66
Coca-Cola, 225
Companies House, 3, 6
Company voluntary arrangement
    (CVA), 203–222, 203–222
  alterations to proposal, 215–216
    index to appendices, 216
    realization of assets, 215–216
  proposals, 206–215
    associated creditors, 211–215
    deferred creditors, 210
    preferential creditors, 209
    secured creditors, 209
    unsecured creditors, 210
Competitors and business, 201
Compound interest, 161
Computerized stock system, 150
Confinity, 7
Contests and free gifts, 182
Continuing professional
    development (CPD), 124
Contractual liabilities, 201
Cookies, 195
Cooking the Books Limited, 24
Corporation tax, 97–98
Cost cutting, 192–193
Cost savings review, 192
Courses and staff training, 124
Court of Appeal, 70
CPD, *see* Continuing professional
    development (CPD)
Credit card, 163
  charges, 127
  facilities, 152–153
  payments, 151, 152–153
Critical illness and health insurance,
    145–147
Critical illness policy, 129
Crowdfunding, 52–53, 242, 243
Current account, 166, 167–168
Current assets, 149–153

cash at bank and in hand, 153
credit card facilities, 152–153
debtors, 151
stock, 149–150
work in progress and
    prepayments, 153
Current liabilities, 154–155
Customer details, 194
CVA, *see* Company voluntary
    arrangement (CVA)

Dasani, 225
Dassler, Adolf, 21
Dassler, Rudolph, 21
Data capture system, 183
Debt crowdfunding, 53
Debtors, 151, 153, 266
Deferred creditors, 210
Deferred taxation, 264
Delayed property transaction, 51
Depreciation, 127–128, 263
Director's loan account, 154–155
Directors responsibilities, 262
Discounts, 187
Dishonesty and business, 201
Dividend returns calculation,
    219–221
Dividends, 30, 94, 96
Dominant customer, 197
Drawdown, *see* Income
    drawdown

eBay, 6–7
EEC, *see* European Economic
    Community (EEC)
EIS, *see* Enterprise Investment
    Scheme (EIS)
Electricity and oil costs, 124
Electronic wallet, 7
E-mail campaigns, 179
E-mail newsletters, 178
Employed individuals, 76
Employers' liability, 70–71

Employment, 75
    concept, 78
    contract, 79–90
    legislation, 70
Employment Appeals Tribunal, 70
Enterprise Investment Scheme
    (EIS), 60–62
Entrepreneurs, 3
Entrepreneurs Relief, 5,
    108–109
Equipment leasing, 125
Equity crowdfunding, 53
Equity instrument, 264
European Court of Justice, 70, 79
European Economic Community
    (EEC), 102
Excel, 34
Expenses, 118, 123–128
Expense sharing partnership, 32
Extra outlets, 189–190

Farming businesses, 230
FDD, *see* Franchise Disclosure
    Document (FDD)
Finance, 49–52
Financial advisors, 240
Financial forecasts, 38
Financial instruments, 264
Financial Reporting Standard for
    Smaller Entities, 262, 263
Financial statements, 263–268
Fixed assets, 131
Fixed rate loan, 142
Fixtures and equipment, 45,
    147–148, 266
Ford Motor Company, 9
Franchise business, 55–56, 190
Franchise Disclosure Document
    (FDD), 56
Freehold *vs.* leasehold property,
    135–138
Free offer vouchers, 193–194
Fry, Arthur, 14

Gearing, 138–140
Geo-marketing, 184–185
Gig economy, 78–79
Global positioning system (GPS)
    tracking, 184
Goodwill, 45–46, 131–133, 171,
    263, 265
    annual percentage rate,
      159–164
    basis of valuation, 144
    critical illness and health
      insurance, 145–147
    current assets, 149–153
    current liabilities, 154–155
    finance/refinance, 141–143
    fixtures and equipment,
      147–148
    freehold *vs.* leasehold, 135–138
    funding of business accounts,
      164–169
    life insurance and endowments,
      144–145
    long-term liabilities, 155–156
    motor vehicles, 148–149
    negative equity and
      valuations, 143
    net assets, 164
    ownership agreement, 140–141
    owning, 140
    purchase of assets and
      equipment, 156–158
    sale and leaseback, 138–140
    type, 134–135
    valuations, 132–133
GPS, *see* Global positioning system
    (GPS) tracking
Guinness, Arthur, 136

Health insurance, critical illness
    and, 145–147
Hire purchase agreement, 157
Hire purchase interest, 128
HM Customs & Excise, 199–200

ICAEW, *see* Institute of Chartered
    Accountants in England
    and Wales (ICAEW)
IHT, *see* Inheritance Tax (IHT)
Il Giornale, 7
Illness, 198–199
Impulse buying, 185–186, 194
Income, 121
    and business, 118
    and expenses, 117–118
    protecting, 128–129
Income drawdown, 236–237, 238
Income tax, 92–97
    dividends, 96
    planning for directors, 96–97
Incorporated business, 29–30,
    59–60
Incorporation process, 171
Individual savings accounts (ISAs),
    232–233
Inheritance Tax (IHT), 63,
    111–113
Innovative finance ISAs, 232
Insolvency
    and liquidators, 201–202
    process, 223
    reasons for, 197–200
Insolvency Act 1986, 209
Institute of Chartered Accountants
    in England and Wales
    (ICAEW), 170
Insurance companies, 194
Insurance costs, 125–126
Intangible fixed assets,
    131, 265
Internet, 186
Investment income, 265

Jobs, Steve, 9, 10
Joint marketing, 182–183
Joint tenants, 137

Konosuke Matsushita, 8

Landline costs, 125
Leasehold property, freehold *vs.*,
    135–138
Lease purchase arrangements, 218
Leeson, Nick, 201
Legal advisors, 172
    expecting from, 172
    knowledgeable, 172
Legal and professional fees, 127
Levchin, Max, 7
Liabilities, 267
Life cover, 129, 237
Life insurance and endowments,
    144–145
Limited company, 29–30, 58–59
Limited liability partnership,
    32–33
Liquid assets, 149
Liquidation, 223–224
Liquidators, insolvency and,
    201–202
Loan repayments, 44, 49–50
Locum cover, 129
Long leasehold property,
    135–136
Long-term liabilities, 155–156
Loyalty cards, 194

Mailings, 178
Market
    experience in, 200
    methods, 183–184, 200
Markkula, Mike, 9–10
Matsushita Electric, 8
Mestral, George de, 15
Minnesota, Mining and
        Manufacturing Company, 14
Mobile payments, 151, 152
The Money Laundry Limited, 24
Mortgages, 163
Motor expenses, 126
Motor vehicles, 148–149
Musk, Elon, 16

National Employment Savings Trust
    (NEST), 68, 241
National insurance, 101, 110–111
National Insurance Employment
    Allowance, 97
National Minimum Wage, 69–77
    employers' liability, 70–71
    employment legislation, 70
    redundancy pay, 74–77
    staff management, 71
    staff relationships, 71–72
    Statutory Adoption Pay, 72–73
    Statutory Maternity Pay, 72–73
    Statutory Paternity Pay, 72–73
    Statutory Shared Parental Pay,
        72–73
    Statutory Sick Pay, 73–74
Negative equity and
        valuations, 143
NEST, *see* National Employment
        Savings Trust (NEST)
Net assets, 164
Networking, 187–188
Nike, 21, 26
Non-building fixed assets, 165
Non-domiciled individuals, 106
Non-specialist accountants, 171
Non-specialist business valuer, 133

Official Records Office, 4
Old pensions, 241
Omidyar, Pierre, 6–7
Online advertising, 180–181
Online business, 20
Operating profit, 265
Ownership agreement, 140–141

Panasonic, 8
Payday loans, 162–164
PAYE system, 66, 72, 75, 77, 78, 111,
        117, 121
Paying-in books, 117
PayPal, 6–7

Peer-to-peer (p2p) lending, *see*
    Debt crowdfunding
Pen Island, 23
Penisland.net, 23
Pensions, 231–239
    annuities, 236, 237–238
    income drawdown, 236–237, 238
    individual savings accounts
        (ISAs), 232–233
    state pension age, 233–236
    tax relief, 238–239
    types, 239–240
Pensions, staff, 67–68
Petty cash, 153
Pfizer, 12
Postage and stationery costs, 125
Post-it note, 14–15
Powergenitalia.com, 23
Preferential creditors, 209, 219–221
Prepayments, 153
Press releases, 180
Pricing and costings, 39–41
Principal's withdrawals, 168–169
Printer toners cost, 125
Privately owned businesses,
    245–247
Private medical insurance, 146
Private Residence Relief, 105
Profit, 128
    and loss account, 121–128, 260,
        267, 269
        expenses, 123–128
        income, 121
    share arrangement, 66
Pro forma employment contract,
    81–85
Pro forma freelance agreement,
    86–90
Property, 45, 133–169
    annual percentage rate, 159–164
    basis of valuation, 144
    critical illness and health
        insurance, 145–147

current assets, 149–153
current liabilities, 154–155
finance/refinance, 141–143
fixtures and equipment, 147–148
freehold *vs.* leasehold, 135–138
funding of business accounts,
    164–169
life insurance and endowments,
    144–145
long-term liabilities, 155–156
motor vehicles, 148–149
negative equity and valuations, 143
net assets, 164
ownership agreement, 140–141
owning, 140
purchase of assets and
    equipment, 156–158
sale and leaseback, 138–140
type, 134–135, 134–135
Property capital, 165
Pull marketing, 186–187
Puma, 21
Purchase and expense invoices, 117
Purchase price, 45–47
Push marketing, 186–187, *see* Direct
    response marketing

Qualifying days (QDs), 73

Receivership, 223
Recruitment costs, 123–124
Redundancy pay, 74–77
Repairs and maintenance, 124–125
Representative APR, 163
Resources, lack of, 200
Retirement and succession, 229–247
    challenge and role in business,
        243–244
    financial advisors, 240
    investing in privately owned
        businesses, 245–247
    investing in someone else's
        business, 242–243

investment, 244–245
NEST, 241
old pensions, 241
passing business to family,
    229–231
pensions, 231–239
    annuities, 236, 237–238
    income drawdown,
        236–237, 238
    individual savings accounts
        (ISAs), 232–233
    state pension age, 233–236
    tax relief, 238–239
    types, 239–240
retirement date, 241–242
Return on investment, 177–178
Revenue Authorities, 72
Rewards and customers, 194

Sale and leaseback arrangement,
    138–140
Sales cost, 59, 123
Sales promotions and marketing
    campaigns, 193–196
Sales split, 58
SAP, *see* Statutory Adoption
    Pay (SAP)
Schultz, Howard, 7
Search engines, 23
Second-level capital acquisitions, 244
Secured creditors, 209
Secured loan, 156
Seed Enterprise Scheme (SEIS), 60,
    63–64
SEIS Reinvestment relief, 64
Self-employed individuals, 76, 77,
    231, 233
Self-employed subcontractors,
    68–69
Self-employment, 75
Self-invested personal pensions
    (SIPPs), 240
Share capital, 267

Share ownership, 30
Short leasehold property, 135–136
ShPP, *see* Statutory Shared Parental
    Pay (ShPP)
Silver, Spencer, 14, 15
SIPPs, *see* Self-invested personal
    pensions (SIPPs)
Small Business Administration, 2, 5
SMP, *see* Statutory Maternity
    Pay (SMP)
Social media, 12, 179
Sole trader approach, 28–29
Solicitors, *see* Legal advisors
Specialist valuers, 133
Speed of Art, 23
Sponsorship and publicity stunts,
    181–182
SPP, *see* Statutory Paternity
    Pay (SPP)
SSP, *see* Statutory Sick Pay (SSP)
Staff costs, 192
Staffing, 65–86
    contract of employment, 79–86
        pro forma, 81–90
    National Minimum Wage, 69–77
        employers' liability, 70–71
        employment legislation, 70
        redundancy pay, 74–77
        staff management, 71
        staff relationships, 71–72
        Statutory Adoption Pay, 72–73
        Statutory Maternity Pay, 72–73
        Statutory Paternity Pay, 72–73
        Statutory Shared Parental Pay,
            72–73
        Statutory Sick Pay, 73–74
    pensions, 67–68
    self-employed subcontractors,
        68–69
    setting wage levels, 66–67
Stakeholder pensions, 239
Stamp Duty Land Tax, 107–108
Starbucks, 7–8

Startup business, 2–4, 244
  government assistance for, 4–6
Statement of affairs, 217–218
State pension age, 233–236
Statutory Adoption Pay (SAP), 72–73
Statutory information, 221–223
Statutory Maternity Pay (SMP),
    72–73
Statutory Paternity Pay (SPP), 72–73
Statutory Shared Parental Pay
    (ShPP), 72–73
Statutory Sick Pay (SSP), 73–74
Stock, 149–150, 263
  and consumables, 47
  records, 118
Stocks and shares ISAs, 232
Subcontract web content, 181
Subscription costs, 125
Sundry expenses, 125
Supermarkets, 41, 185, 198
Supervisor fees and remuneration,
    212–213

Tangible fixed assets, 131, 263, 266
Tax allowances, 148
Taxation, 29, 52, 265
Tax Authorities, 28, 64, 75–77,
    91, 98, 107, 108, 115, 119,
    129–130, 133, 150, 242
Taxes, 91–113
  agricultural relief, 113
  Annual Tax on Enveloped
    Dwellings (ATED), 106–107
  capital allowances, 110
  capital gains, 103–106
    for people non-domiciled in
      UK, 106
    rates and bands, 105
    rules, 104–105
  corporation, 97–98
  enquiries, 129–130
  Entrepreneurs' Relief, 108–109

income, 92–97
  dividends, 96
  planning for directors, 96–97
Inheritance Tax, 111–113
issues, 54
legislation, 44–45
national insurance, 110–111
payment, 168–169
planning exercise, 98–99
relief, 57, 60, 142, 157, 238–239
saving, 271
  scheme, 30
Stamp Duty Land Tax, 107–108
value-added, 102–103
  rates, 103
year one, 99–100
year three, 100–102
year two, 100
Tax man and source of capital,
    199–200
Tesla, 16
Training, 56, 66
Transactions, 43, 152, 154, 268
Turnaround companies, 244–245
Turnover, 263

Uber, 79
UK Supreme Court, 70, 79
Unaudited statutory financial
    statements, 258–259
Unemployment/redundancy, 13
Unique selling point (USP), 18–19
Unsecured creditors, 210, 219–221
Unsecured loan, 156
USP, *see* Unique selling point (USP)

Valuation, 132–133, 143–144
Value-added tax (VAT), 47–48,
    102–103
Velcro, 15
Viagra, 12
Virgin, 224

Virgin Cola, 224
Voluntary arrangement, 202,
      223–224
Wages
  records, 117
  and salaries, 123
Water rates, 124
Web-hosting services, 180
Website, 175–177

Work from home, 124
Working capital, 155,
      165–166
Work in progress provision, 153
Wozniak, Steve, 9

YouTube, 20

Zero-hours contracts, 28, 77

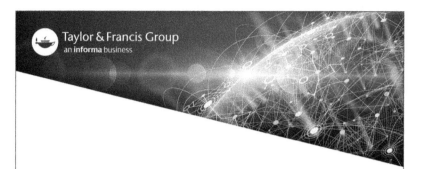

For Product Safety Concerns and Information please contact our EU
representative GPSR@taylorandfrancis.com
Taylor & Francis Verlag GmbH, Kaufingerstraße 24, 80331 München, Germany